DODGE PICKUP
COLOR HISTORY

Don Bunn & Mike Mueller

Motorbooks International
Publishers & Wholesalers

First published in 1996 by Motorbooks International
Publishers & Wholesalers, 729 Prospect Avenue, PO Box 1,
Osceola, WI 54020-0001 USA

Motorbooks International books are also available at
discounts in bulk quantity for industrial or sales-promotional
use. For details write to Special Sales Manager at the
Publisher's address

Printed in Hong Kong

Library of Congress Cataloging-in-Publication Data
Bunn, Don.
  Dodge pickups color history/Don Bunn, Mike Mueller.
  p. cm.
  Includes index.
  ISBN 0-7603-0170-0 (pbk. : alk. paper)
  1. Dodge trucks--History. I. Mueller, Mike.
  II. Title.
TL230.5.D63B762   1996
629.223--dc20   96-14080

On the front cover: The most popular pickups collected by
Dodge enthusiasts are those built between 1939 and 1947.
This unrestored, original-condition 1940 VC half-ton pickup
belongs to Ron Cenowa of Shelby Township, Michigan.

On the frontispiece: The stylized charging ram hood ornament
on Ron Cenowa's 1949 half-ton pickup.

On the title page: This 1946 one-ton WD-21 truck, owned by
Ron Cenowa, has a factory-installed 9ft stake body. The 1946
one-ton trucks retained the same cab style as the 1942
models and were powered by a 230ci 105hp L-6 engine.

On the back cover: Two great Dodge pickup styles. The finned
1957 D100 Sweptside, owned by Dan Topping of Tifton,
Georgia, was created to compete with Chevrolet's Cameo
Carrier and Ford's Ranchero. The 1996 Dodge Ram, courtesy
of Dodge Division, Chrysler Corporation, continues the
company's revolutionary pickup design introduced in 1994.

Contents

Acknowledgments

Many individuals across the years helped make this *Dodge Pickup Color History* possible, including members from the American Truck Historical Society, the Turbo Diesel Register, and the former Light Commercial Vehicle Association.

Chrysler Corporation provided color photos in addition to those Mike Mueller shot, and the company provided most of the black-and-white photos too. I also want to recognize Stan Holtzman of Los Angeles for providing a color photo of an interesting and unusual big Dodge diesel truck of the seventies.

My good friends Tom Brownell and Monty Montgomery played key roles, for which I am deeply indebted.

Mike Mueller and I thank and acknowledge the following owners for allowing us to photograph their trucks: Steve Fisher of Somerset, Kentucky, 1937 commercial panel; Ron Cenowa of Shelby Township, Michigan, 1940 half-ton pickup, 1946 one-ton stake, 1947 one and a half-ton cab-over-engine tractor, and 1949 half-ton pickup; Bill Garland of Carlisle, Pennsylvania, 1947 Power Wagon; Dan and Beth Schaffer of St. Paul, Minnesota, 1954 half-ton Truck-O-Matic pickup; Bruce Welle of Sauk Centre, Minnesota, 1957 W200 Power Wagon pickup; Dan Topping of Tifton, Georgia, 1957 D100 Sweptside; George Rabuse of St. Paul, Minnesota, 1963 M37B1 four-wheel-drive Army truck; Greg Tomberlin of Brainerd, Minnesota, 1965 D100 Custom Sports Special pickup; Dennis Guest of Lockport, Illinois, 1968 A100 compact pickup; Ken and Carol Merten of St. Cloud, Minnesota, 1969 D100 half-ton pickup, 1978 Li'l Red Express Truck, and 1990 Li'l Red Dakota pickup; Dale and Phyllis Birtles of Hudson, Michigan, 1989 Dodge Cummins turbo diesel pickup; Jimmy Scarry of Floral Park, New York, 1989 Dodge Cummins turbo diesel pickup; Dodge Division Chrysler Corporation, 1994 Ram SLT Laramie V-8 pickup.

I am always interested in hearing from Dodge truck owners. If you would like to contact me, please do so at: 5109 West 105th Street, Bloomington, MN 55437, or phone at (612) 831-2309.

Thank you.

Don Bunn

Introduction and Trends

Popularity of Dodge trucks among collectors has been growing rapidly for the past decade or more. There has always been a core group of dedicated Dodge truck aficionados who have quietly collected, restored, and enjoyed their bits of Dodge history, but fortunately, for the past ten years or more their numbers have been multiplying.

The historic turnaround of the Chrysler Corporation has contributed significantly to the rise in interest in Chrysler products and to Dodge trucks in particular. Interest in Dodge trucks began to increase dramatically when Dodge Truck and Cummins Engine Company came together to install Cummins' best-in-class midrange diesel engine, affectionately called the Super B, in Dodge pickups. It has been heartwarming to see normally ultraconservative truck owners immediately switch allegiances and take to Dodge Cummins pickups like ducks to water.

Hard on the heels of the Dodge Cummins phenomenon was Chrysler's important introduction of the world-class Dodge full-size T300 pickup in midyear 1993 as a 1994 model truck—a truck that has set new design, power, and quality standards for large pickups. Chrysler Corporation's people outdid themselves when they created this critically new product. The T300 may go down in Chrysler's history as the company's most important new product ever.

Credit for the success of the T300 has to go to Mr. Bob Lutz, Chrysler president. Bob Lutz is a truck man as well as a product man. Chrysler's Platform Team concept, which was responsible for developing the T300, was his idea. He empowered his people by encouraging them to bring every bit of their creativity and energy to the team. The team concept created a culture that enabled all disciplines to work together. There were no "stars," rather all members worked as one. By totally focusing on their common goal, the platform team made it happen.

Dodge Truck had been in the pits for so long, some Chrysler employees had lost sight of the fact that they could be and would be the industry's pickup leader. A former two-way race for full-size pickup sales suddenly became a three-way race when Dodge Truck's large new full-size pickup assembly plant in St. Louis, Missouri, came on-line in midyear 1995. This plant is programmed to build up to 60 percent of its production in Club Cab models.

Another vehicle that played a big part in Dodge Truck's comeback was the industry's only midsize truck, the Dakota pickup. The Dakota was launched in 1986 as a 1987 model-year truck. Because Dodge was the last player to launch a less than full-size pickup, engineers had the important advantage of studying and analyzing all other products—both domestic and imported—before launching their new downsized truck. Dodge management agreed that a truck a bit bigger than compact trucks but smaller than full-size trucks was the right size.

In the beginning, Dakota, code named "N" truck, was a co-venture with Chrysler's Japanese partner, Mitsubishi Motors. Mitsubishi later dropped out of the program because the Dakota was too big to sell in Japan. Its size would have subjected it to a higher tax rate than taxes on existing Toyota and Nissan minitrucks. Chrysler management saw merit in the N-truck program for America and went ahead without Mitsubishi.

Dakota was a winner from the beginning. Later additions of a Club Cab model and superlative performance from Magnum V-6 and V-8 engines caused Dakota's sales to boom. Buyers discovered that the Dakota was a more powerful truck than either competitor's full-size half-ton trucks, yet it supplied more than adequate cab space, payload capacity, and towing performance in a tidy package better suited to buyers' needs.

Dodge began using hard-charging ram's head hood ornaments for its trucks in 1933. This highly stylized ram graces the front of a 1947 stake truck.

Collectability Trends

Collecting Dodge trucks can be fun. The problem for someone getting started is what to zero in on because there is so much to choose from. A word of caution if you are just getting started: Study Dodge truck history a bit before opening your checkbook. There is nothing wrong, however, if you sometimes let your heart be your guide. If you want a plain Jane Dodge pickup like the one you remember from your family's farm, it is the right truck for you. If you have fond memories of family vacation trips in a mid-sixties Dodge A100 Sportsman Wagon and know of a similar one in good condition offered for sale, that may be the truck for you.

What makes Dodge truck collecting so much fun is the broad scope of Dodge truck collectability. Dodge trucks date back to 1918, making many years, models, and types available. Over the years, Dodge truck models have included trucks from half-ton com-

mercials to heavy-duty three-, four-, and five-ton models. Plus, there have been all those interesting, exclusive, and unique special Dodge models: Graham Brothers trucks; double-level panels of the thirties; military trucks; Power Wagons; B series Spring Special Pickups; Custom Sports Specials; Adult Toys; A100 vans, wagons, and pickups; cab-over-engines; Hemi V-8-powered medium- and heavy-duty trucks; and so on. Fortunately, there is a collector for every type, style, and age truck ever built.

Recently, a growing interest in restoring 1933 to 1935 Glamour-era commercial pickups has surfaced. Mechanical parts for these trucks can be found, but body parts are rare. Collectors are showing an increased interest in all models from the Sweptline era of 1961 to 1971. Again, mechanical parts for these trucks are readily available, but body parts are getting rare; you'll have to work a bit to find them. Unfortunately, these trucks were rust-prone.

Military trucks from 1940 to 1968 are hot. Military Dodge collectors are somewhat of a dedicated subculture. Power Wagons, the original military style from 1946 to 1968, have a large and growing following. Power Wagon mechanical and body parts are readily available. Collecting standard cab Power Wagons beginning with 1957 up to 1980 are coming on strong. Especially the 1950s- and 1960s-era Power Wagon Town Panel and Town Wagon models. Among the hottest Dodge collectibles are the huge Dodge Bighorn tractors built between 1973 and 1975. Big trucks are not for everyone because they require special storage facilities. Restoring a huge diesel tractor also gets to be a bit spendy.

Standbys continue to be the W series trucks from the Job-Rated era of 1939 to 1947. More of these trucks are in the hands of collectors than any other series. Panels, pickups, canopies, and stakes from this era are all excellent choices, and interestingly, collector attention to medium- and heavy-duty W series trucks is also picking up steam. In second place in popularity with collectors are the B series Pilot-House-era trucks built between 1948 and 1953. C series Functional Design era trucks of 1954 to 1956 are also gaining a lot of interest. Parts, mechanical and sheet metal, for any of these series are available.

Collecting Tips

I'd like to leave you with a couple of tips regarding collecting Dodge trucks. First, for those of you who are looking for a truck but don't have a particular model in mind, look for a rare model. A rare model can be an otherwise ordinary pickup, but one with an automatic transmission, for example. Rare trucks are not limited to flashy, high-visibility Sweptsides, Custom Sports Specials, Li'l Red Express Trucks, and so on. The Truck-O-Matic 1954 half-ton is an excellent example of a rare truck. To my knowledge, only four are known to exist, two in Minnesota, one in North Dakota, and the fourth in Indiana, but surely there are many others. Other rare trucks include those with fluid drive, a long wheelbase 1953 half-ton pickup, the first half-ton built by the Big Three with a long cargo box, cab-over-engine models, Route Vans, and trucks that were the first model to have special or new equipment, such as the first V-8 engine or first automatic transmission. There are countless other examples which you can discover by doing a little research. Hunting for a rare truck can be fun in itself.

Second, consider low-mileage, original-condition trucks. These trucks often still have their original mufflers and tires. Once acquired, you only need to "detail" them as there is no need for a complete restoration. These trucks are a real link to the past as they are what they are; they leave no questions of what specific details should have been. Once you have paid the seller's asking price, you will not be faced with large future expenses because nothing but detailing will be required. Be assured there are many trucks of this type available. Be patient and be picky; they are out there.

The 1918 Dodge Brothers roadster pickup is a good example of early commercial vehicle production. The factory supplied a chassis cab and the buyer or dealer supplied the body. Dodge did not offer a factory-built pickup until 1924. *Glen Campbell*

Chapter 1

The Early Years
1916–1932

The Dodge brothers were not interested in building a car with their name on it; they were perfectly content with being the industry's leading manufacturer of automotive parts.

Dodge Brothers Trucks, 1916–1928

John F. and Horace E. Dodge were sons of a Niles, Michigan, machinist. The brothers possessed considerable mechanical aptitude and learned the machinist's trade from their father, who ran a shop specializing in internal combustion engines for marine use. They left tiny Niles, located in the far southwestern corner of the state, in 1886 and eventually settled in Detroit where they worked as machinists at the Murphy Boiler Works until 1894. Later, they moved across the border to Windsor, Ontario, where they worked as machinists for the Canadian Typography Company.

Before long they began to manufacture precision metal products. Horace invented a four-point, dirt-proof, adjustable bicycle ball bearing, and in 1897 the brothers established the Evans and Dodge Bicycle Company with Fred Evans. In 1900, they sold their part of the bicycle company and returned to Detroit.

The brothers opened a machine shop with twelve employees and began building auto parts for the fledgling, but rapidly growing, automotive industry. A reputation for excellent workmanship was quickly established, and orders began to pour into the company, forcing them to move to a larger building in Detroit.

The Dodge brothers worked in tandem, each with his unique talents. Both were astute businessmen, but John was the more talkative and aggressive, while Horace was the mechanical genius who tended to be quiet and easygoing. The brothers worked together and played together; whatever they did, they did with great vigor. They established a reputation for partying and drinking, which they engaged in as hard as they did their work.

The Dodge brothers were in the inner circle when Henry Ford organized his fledgling company to build the world's first low-priced volume automobile. Rejecting all offers from the other manufacturers, they joined Henry Ford's new venture by agreeing to supply Ford with 650 chassis, including engines, transmissions, and axles, for $250 each. This began a profitable but stormy relationship between the two firms. The contract kept the 150 Dodge employees fully occupied, and the Dodges began working exclusively for Ford. Ford built a plant on Detroit's Mack Avenue to assemble cars from parts made elsewhere. His entire operation was dependent upon extensive credit from his parts suppliers. Investing $10,000 ($7,000 in materials and a $3,000 bank note), the Dodge brothers became a one-tenth owner (100 shares) in the Ford Motor Company, incorporated on June 16, 1903. Dodge delivered its first shipment of chassis to the Mack Avenue plant in July via horse-drawn hayracks, and Ford assembled his first cars.

Dodge quality quickly earned Ford products a reputation for quality and reliability, which caused Ford's volume to mushroom. Upon filling Ford's first order for 650 chassis, he ordered another 755 for delivery January through May 1904 and insisted on the right to order 500 more by early April. By the spring of 1905, when Ford moved into his new Piquette Avenue plant, the Dodge brothers supplied 400 engines and transmissions per month. Dodge continued as the major supplier, but by late 1905 Ford was already taking steps to produce his own engines and transmissions for the low-priced Model N.

Seeing the handwriting on the wall, the brothers purchased a 30-acre tract of land in Hamtramck, Michigan (located within the city of Detroit), and began building a major manufacturing complex to supply Ford. In 1912 they supplied Ford with 180,000 transmission-axle sets, with future prospects for much larger orders.

The appearance of this excellently restored 1920 Dodge Brothers screenside is typical of all screensides built from 1918 through 1922. The screenside's dependability established Dodge trucks as the industry standard.

The Dodge brothers did not want to be completely dependent upon one customer, so they gave the required one year's notice to Ford that they would terminate their contract effective August 1914. They retained the stock they had held since 1903, which had been very profitable for them. Through 1914, they earned $3.8 million in dividends from their stock and earned another $1.7 million in profits on Ford business. When Ford ceased to pay dividends to stockholders in 1916, the Dodges brought suit, which forced Ford to pay a dividend of slightly more than $19 million in 1918. Ten percent of this went to the Dodges. Ford bought out the other stockholders of the Ford Motor Company in July 1919, giving the Dodge brothers $25 million for their 10 percent stake in the company. All told with dividends, profits, and the sale of the stock, the brothers realized a return of about $32 million on their 1903 investment of $10,000. Henry Ford was both the reason for their huge plant in Hamtramck and the source of funds with which to build it. Before their own car was announced, the brothers had built the mechanical parts for at least half a million automobiles.

Signing up quality car dealerships was not a problem for the Dodges, as they received a total of 22,000 requests for dealerships. While the Dodge name was not well known by the general public, industry people knew it well, and many dealers who knew the fine reputation of the Dodges wanted to be part of their new venture. Normally, a start-up car manufacturer had to go hunting for whatever dealers it could, but in the case of the Dodge brothers, they simply chose the best applicants and immediately built a successful dealer network.

The first official notification to the public of the brothers' plans was a small advertisement without illustrations, except for their corporate logo, in the August 29, 1914, edition of *Saturday Evening Post*. It read, "Dodge Brothers, Detroit, who have manufactured the vital parts for more than 500,000 motor cars will this fall market a car bearing their own name."

The Dodge brothers knew Ford's Model T very well because they built all of it except for its body, wheels, and tires. They figured they could build a higher-quality, larger, more powerful, and dependable car for only a slightly higher price. The brothers set out to engineer a car to fit this description and have it ready by July 1, 1914, when Dodge's Ford contract would expire.

The first Dodge cars were ready for sale in November 1914 and were regarded as 1915 models. Its 212ci, L-head four-cylinder engine developed 30 to 35 horsepower (hp), which was considerably higher than the Model T's and was a major factor in competing against Ford a few short years later in the commercial car business. An unusual feature of the new Dodge was its combined starter-generator unit. Driven by a silent chain from the crankshaft, the starter was automatically set in motion when the armature voltage fell below the battery voltage. The battery was a 12-volt with 40-amp capacity. Clutch was of the cone leather type. Transmission was a three-speed with a gear arrangement in an unorthodox shift pattern, which was the opposite from the accepted stan-

dard H pattern. Another unusual feature of the new Dodge four-passenger touring car, the only model offered, was its all-steel body, which was rare for its time. Equipped with genuine leather seats, the brothers priced their outstanding new car at only $785.

Dodge Brothers was always in the enviable position of not being able to build all the cars the public was willing to buy, a fact that remained true almost up to the moment Walter Chrysler purchased Dodge in July 1928. Dodge's huge Hamtramck plant was equipped with all the required machinery and facilities for machining, forging, and casting all the components used in manufacturing cars except for bodies, tires, and window glass. The Dodges built their own engines from blocks cast on site, as well as frames, axles, and transmissions. However, the plant had never assembled entire cars. An assembly

When Walter Chrysler purchased Dodge in 1928, he inherited the company's 1929 truck models, which went on sale July 1, 1928. Shown here is a 1929 half-ton chassis cowl. Because

Dodge had converted all car production to six-cylinder engines, all 1929 Dodge trucks were powered by six-cylinder engines.

Dodge Brothers' 1929 half-ton Merchants Express pickup retained the vestibule cab (small window behind cab doors), which was typical of the Graham Brothers' cab style. This truck's drivetrain consisted of a 208ci, 63hp L-head engine mated to a three-speed transmission.

plant was constructed with a production line of sorts. It took some time for the plant to learn the fine art of car assembly, which it soon mastered, and slowly daily production rates began to rise.

Almost from the beginning of car production, dealers and satisfied customers urged management to add commercial vehicles. At this time in the development of motor cars, a dependable automobile was a rare thing and a dependable commercial vehicle was even rarer. The Dodge brothers resisted adding commercials for the simple reason they were unable to build all the cars the public wanted.

Two events pushed the brothers over the line, events over which they had no control. Less than two years after the first Dodge automobile rolled off Hamtramck's production line, the U.S. Army chose Dodge touring sedans to make the world's first mechanized attack against an armed enemy. This event took place in northern Mexico immediately south of its border with the United States. Young Lieutenant George S. Patton, Jr., loaded up three Dodge tourings with fifteen soldiers and attacked the Mexicans' fortified desert position. At-

tacking at 40 miles per hour (mph), Patton and his men reached the enemy, before they knew what was going on. The suddenness with which Patton and his men swooped down on them confused the enemy, causing them to lose before they even began to fight. Lieutenant Patton later commented, "The motor car is the modern war horse."

Patton's commander at the Mexican border was none other than General "Black Jack" Pershing. Pershing led the U.S. forces in battling Mexican General Pancho Villa. Even though he was the head of 10,000 cavalrymen, Pershing pursued the enemy with his swift Dodge tourings. Before the campaign ended, Pershing placed orders for close to 250 more Dodge cars.

The second event that forced the Dodge brothers to build commercial cars was America's involvement in World War I. When General Pershing went to France in 1917 as commander of the American Expeditionary Forces, his Dodge went with him. Remembering the effectiveness, toughness, and dependability of his Dodge war machines in Mexico, he ordered thousands of military Dodges for the Army. These consisted of a combination of tourings, roadsters, and chassis cowl units beefed up for severe service and fitted with various types of military bodies: ambulances, light repair vehicles, screensides, cargo trucks, and so on. Exact quantities are not known, but it is estimated the Army purchased a total of about 20,000 Dodge vehicles of all types for World War I. Many of these Dodge cars and trucks continued to serve the military into the 1930s.

With the end of the war, Dodge was, in effect, in the commercial car business. The 114-inch (in) Dodge automobile chassis had been engineered with stronger parts to accept the screenside body and a maximum payload of 1,000 pounds (lb) (half-ton), and the screenside body, nearly identical to that used by the Army, was available from Budd. Dodge's four-cylinder engine, transmission, and front-end sheet metal did not require modification.

In 1917, there were major differences between a commercial car and a truck. A commercial car was an automobile chassis, without any modification or with slight modification, with a delivery body fitted. A truck, on the other hand, was built from the wheels up for severe usage, that is, with a strong ladder-type frame, heavy axles, springs, transmissions, wheels, and tires.

Dodge Brothers' first screenside was assembled in mid-October 1917, priced at $885. The company's first panel followed on March 26, 1918, priced at $935. The panel was the same size as the screenside and was also rated for a 1,000lb maximum payload capacity. Vital statistics of the first commercial: 114in wheelbase; shipping weight (screenside), 2,610lb; four-cylinder, 212ci, L-head engine rated at 35 brake horsepower; body loading space, 72in long, 43in wide, and 54in high; hickory spoke wheels with 33x4in tires, front and rear, plain tread front and nonskid rears; driver's seat upholstered in genuine leather; open C-cab with sloping roof, driver's compartment open to the load compartment; and roll curtains protected the load compartment and the driver's compartment.

Dodge called its screenside body an "express." This term was used to differentiate a small, commercial from a truck. Trucks in those days were chain driven and equipped with solid rubber wheels. For these reasons, trucks were very slow. Rough roads of cobblestones, or worse, would shake a truck apart, if it would have been capable of high speeds. Commercials, on the other hand, rode on balloon tires and were propelled by an automobile-type driveshaft capable of speeds up to 35mph, which was downright fast for the time. Light loads were logically delivered in the faster "express" vehicles. Much commerce of the day was still delivered by four-legged horsepower.

Because Dodge Brothers' commercial cars were passenger car-based vehicles, commercials changed in style and engineering appointments over the years only when changes were made in Dodge Brothers' automobiles. From the day the first Dodge passenger car was built, it was Dodge Brothers' stated philosophy to integrate changes and improvements in the product as soon as they were available, frequently without publicizing the fact, and often changes were not visible. As a matter of fact, only on two occasions were changes of this nature readily apparent.

Four distinct types of Dodge Brothers' commercial cars are recognized. Type One screenside began in October 1917, and the panel in March 1918. Hallmarks of Type One commercials were their 114in wheelbase cowl and low radiator. The commercials' front sheet metal styling back to the windshield cowl was the same as that of Dodge passenger cars for the same years. Type One commercials continued in production until May 1922; however, a large number of improvements were made during their almost five-year run, most of which were unseen.

Type Two commercials began in May 1922 and ran until the end of June 1923, basically the 1923 model year. Dodge Brothers model year began on July 1 and ended on June 30. Styling changes included raising the radiator, cowl, and hood 3-1/2in. The commercials' windshields were slanted, and an outside door handle was added on the driver's side. All Dodge commercials were painted black.

The factory built only two body-type commercials—screenside and panel; however, taxis and commercial chassis on which special bodies were mounted by the customer were also counted in total production.

Type Three models began in July 1923 and ran until the end of June 1925 for the panel and until the end of September 1925 for the screenside. Maximum payload capacity was increased to 1,500lb (three-quarter-ton) due to a 2in longer wheelbase, longer rear springs, and an enlarged body. Overall appearance remained basically the same as that of Type Two vehicles.

Type Four Dodge Brothers commercial cars featured the first entirely enclosed cab with roll-down glass door windows. A closed cab was a welcomed change for those owners who lived in colder parts of the country. Closed cabs, too, gave them a more modern appearance than the former open C-type cab. Steel disc wheels also added a more modern appearance than the former wooden spoke wheels.

One new model was added to the Type Four commercial lineup, the 140in wheelbase 8ft panel. While still a three-quarter-ton truck, it could handle light but bulky loads.

Other engineering advancements of note ushered in during Type Four's production included changing the transmission to one with a standard H gearshift pattern, adding the smoother five-bearing crankshaft engine, and the famous two-unit North East 12-volt electrical system gave way to a 6-volt North East system.

The Type Four commercial panel ran until the end of June 1926, and the screenside ran until the beginning of September 1926. These dates did not signal the end for these trucks, rather these were the dates when production was turned over to Dodge Brothers' wholly owned truck-building subsidiary, Graham Brothers. Commercial cars and all larger models were renamed Graham Brothers, and truck production was entirely moved out of Dodge Main. Commercials continued to be built right up to the time Walter Chrysler purchased Dodge. It just so happens that it also coincided with the end of production of Dodge's famous four-cylinder engine. From that point on, Dodge built only six-cylinder engines.

Early Chrysler-Built Trucks, 1929–1932

Walter Chrysler's timing on closing the deal to acquire Dodge Brothers, Inc., corresponded exactly with the 1929 model year introduction (July 1, 1928). Chrysler's men lost no time in taking control of Dodge Brothers' huge Dodge Main manufacturing complex in Hamtramck, Michigan, for they had lusted over this world-class facility for months, but there was absolutely nothing they could do about the Dodge Brothers/Graham Brothers 1929 model year vehicles. Dodge Brothers properties were scattered from southern Indiana, where the Graham Brothers truck body factory was located in Evansville, to other facilities in Detroit other than Dodge Main, Dodge's Canadian factory, and facilities in England belonging to Dodge Brothers (Britain) Limited. Getting their arms around this huge enterprise kept Mr. Chrysler and his men busy for many months. Chrysler's men were eager to get their hands on the Graham Brothers huge truck cab and body-building plant in Evansville, which for years had built all Graham Brothers standard and special cabs and truck bodies.

Chrysler's purchase of Dodge Brothers instantly put his company in the truck business in a big way. For the 1929 model year, Graham Brothers' truck line ran the gamut from a half-ton, light, and fast Merchants Express 6-1/2ft panel to three-ton heavy-duty trucks. In addition, school buses, parlor coaches, club coaches, and streetcar coaches were an important part of the Graham Brothers' total business.

The most historically interesting feature of Graham Brothers' 1929 line was the fact that all trucks from half-ton to three-ton were powered by six-cylinder engines. The reason was simple: Dodge Brothers no longer built a four-cylinder-powered automobile. Every Dodge automobile for 1929 was six-cylinder powered. Dodge's famous four-cylinder engine had been the cornerstone of the company since the first Dodge car was built in 1914. The famous four played an important role in the success of Dodge commercial vehicles, too. Every one was powered by the original Dodge four-cylinder engine, from the first half-ton Dodge commercial screenside and panel trucks built in 1917 to the last of the original-type Dodge Brothers screensides and panels built in mid-year 1928, just prior to Chrysler's purchase (wearing Graham Brothers nameplates and rated at three-quarter-ton capacity).

Graham Brothers' half-ton SD Fast Four panel delivery, which was a new model in 1928, changed considerably for 1929. First of all, the new model, now called a Merchants Express SE (still a panel truck), was repowered from a four- to a six-cylinder engine. Wheelbase was stretched 2in to 110in, even though the pan-

el's appearance did not change. The other major engineering refinement in this truck was the changeover to four-wheel hydraulic brakes from the previous arrangement of rear-wheel-only mechanical brakes. One can only imagine the improved performance delivered from the six-cylinder engine and the stopping power delivered by four-wheel hydraulic brakes.

The SE's six-cylinder engine was exceptionally smooth because of its seven-bearing crankshaft and aluminum pistons. Horsepower developed was 58 from a 208ci piston displacement. Power for the long hard pull, flashing acceleration, ample top speed, and dependability were its hallmarks. Transmission was a three-speed. The rear axle ratio was 4.455:1.

The Merchants Express' panel body's loading space was a full 68in long by 44-1/2in wide and 44in high. Payload capacity was 1,000lb.

Riding on a 120in wheelbase chassis and featuring Graham Brothers styling with double moldings beneath cab door windows, the new three-quarter-ton series looked more trucklike than the former automobile-based three-quarter-ton series. These trucks were powered by the same 208ci, 58hp six-cylinder L-head engine used in the Merchants Express models. Four-wheel hydraulic brakes were standard equipment, too. Other specifications included: three-speed transmission, wood spoke wheels, 7ft body lengths, and spare tire carrier located under the frame at the rear.

The final new 1929 light-duty model was the one-ton series. Styling of the one-ton series was the same as that of the commercial trucks with setback front axles and double moldings under cab door windows. Major specifications included: 130in wheelbase; 208ci, 58hp L-head six-cylinder engine; four-speed transmission; four-wheel hydraulic brakes; steel spoke wheels with 30x5 eight-ply tires front and rear; and 8ft body lengths on pickup, stake, platform, and farm box. The panel was 9ft long.

Payload capacities on all truck series corresponded with their tonnage rating; for example, half-ton was 1,000lb, three-quarter-ton was 1,500lb, one and a half-ton was 3,000lb, and so on.

Medium- and heavy-duty one and a half-ton, two-ton, and three-ton models were restyled in the same manner as light-duty models. One and a half-ton trucks were powered by the 208ci, six-cylinder engine; two-ton and three-ton trucks were powered by the 242ci, 78hp L-head six-cylinder engine. All models featured four-speed transmissions and four-wheel hydraulic brakes.

Early in January 1929, Chrysler announced that effective immediately its entire line of Graham Brothers' commercial cars, trucks, buses, and motor coaches would be marketed under the Dodge Brothers' name. However, Dodge did not begin attaching a Dodge Brothers nameplate to their trucks until 1932. Truck distribution remained with Dodge dealers only.

Dodge's half-ton Merchants Express panel was the only half-ton in the low-priced market with six-cylinder power, which was both good and bad. Good in that its greater power and performance positioned it above all competition, but the added cost of the six-cylinder engine priced it above the competition. Management was forced to re-engineer the half-ton Merchants Express for the third time in less than two years. When introduced in May 1929, the new model was priced at $545. It was the lowest-priced chassis ever offered by Dodge. The new, roomy and attractive panel body was priced at $795 (without bumpers or spare tire), compared to $845 for the half-ton panel it replaced. Dodge engineers replaced the six with the "Plymouth" four-cylinder, 175.4ci, 45hp L-head engine. This engine was originally a Maxwell Motor Company engine, the auto company Walter Chrysler reorganized into the Chrysler Corporation in 1925. The new panel featured four-wheel hydraulic brakes, 109in wheelbase, 20in wooden wheels, and a three-speed transmission.

Style-wise, the new Merchants Express was almost identical to the former panel. The tradition of painting

light-duty trucks blue with cream wheels, black hubs, and black fenders continued. The panel's interior was finished in gray.

Chrysler Corporation's management aggressively pursued additional truck business in 1930 by re-engineering its one-ton truck line. First, it introduced a new four-cylinder-powered (the "Plymouth" engine) one-ton series. Offered in chassis cab and seven body types, the new one-ton trucks featured four-cylinder power, four-wheel hydraulic brakes, and a truck-type four-speed transmission. Wheelbase was increased 3in to 133in over the former one-ton series, and prices were reduced by $250. The new trucks reached dealers' showrooms in September, but were considered 1930 models.

Dodge Truck designers were very concerned with the styling of their trucks, rightly believing that business owners cared about their trucks' appearance. Customers judged a business by the truck that delivered the

Three-quarter-ton 1931 models are extremely rare because Dodge offered them, but they were not cataloged. Wheelbase

of this panel was 124in; inside body loading length was 78in. Engine was the 208ci, 63hp L-head six cylinder.

Dodge Brothers' 1929 half-ton Merchants Express panel rode on a 110in wheelbase chassis. The engine was the same 208ci L-head as used in the pickup. Spoke wheels were standard equipment; tires were 29x5.00 six-ply balloon-type, front and rear. Note the absence of a small window behind the cab door, which indicates Chrysler's styling influence. This truck, like all Chrysler-built automobiles, was equipped with four-wheel hydraulic brakes.

owner's goods. Dodge advertising claimed that, "The handsome appearance of Dodge Brothers trucks therefore has a definite advertising and business building value." The new one-ton was styled in the manner of the half-ton Merchants Express line. The handsome new Dodge trucks no longer looked like an automobile from the front and like a truck from the rear. Dodge truck bodies were built in the former Graham Brothers truck body plant in Evansville. Body choices included pickup, panel, stake, screen, canopy, farm, and platform. All bodies had 8ft of loading space.

The same 133in wheelbase chassis was offered with a 208ci, 63hp, L-head six-cylinder engine. With the same body choices, or chassis cab only, the six sold for $100 more than the comparable four-cylinder model. Dodge continued to build the 140in wheelbase one-ton series, but it still featured the old cab style, as did all other Dodge trucks from one and a half-ton to three-ton capacity.

With the Great Depression entering its second year, Dodge Truck's management challenge was to keep costs under control and offer customers the best possible values. Management divided its truck line into two groups. The Standard Line consisted of light-duty models ranging from half-ton to one and a half-ton trucks. The Heavy-Duty Line consisted of models ranging from a heavy one and a half-ton to three-ton trucks. Prices on the Standard Line tumbled. A new 136in wheelbase one and a half-ton model was priced at only $595 for a chassis cab with four-cylinder engine and single rear wheels. The body, six-cylinder engine, and dual rear wheels were extra-cost. The half-ton panel's price was lowered to $645. The six-cylinder engine sold for $100 more whether in a half-ton or one and a half-ton truck.

Another interesting change for 1931 was that of changing all model descriptions from a name, such as Merchants Express or Three-Ton, to a system of letters and numbers. Dodge renamed its entire truck line the F

This 1931 Dodge half-ton pickup's style was typical for all half-ton models through 1932. Dodge made this truck avail-able with either a four- or a six-cylinder engine. Payload was 1,000lb.

series. For example, a UF10 was a four-cylinder half-ton; without the U prefix it was a six-cylinder half-ton. An F62A was a three-ton with straight frame rails.

The 1932 model trucks carried over without change for the most part, but that does not mean management sat still. Dodge trucks for 1932 were available with four-, six-, and eight-cylinder engines. The four was the "Plymouth" engine, sixes were former Dodge Brothers engines, and the eight was shared with eight-cylinder Chrysler Imperial automobiles. With the 385ci,

120hp eight-cylinder engine, Dodge trucks moved up to the four-ton range, a first for Dodge. The G-80 four-ton was rated for a maximum GCW rating of 50,000lb in tractor-trailer service.

The balance of the line remained as before, except for a new one and a half-ton lower-priced model. It was a four-cylinder-powered UG-30 model with a 131in wheelbase priced at only $525 for chassis cab, which was only $30 more than a Ford Model A with the same wheelbase.

Chapter 2

Beauty and Dependability Models
1933–1938

The year 1933 was one of new beginnings for Dodge Truck Division, and for the entire Chrysler Corporation. Up to this time, Dodge trucks built by Chrysler were essentially the same in style and engineering as the trucks built under the former regimes of the Dodge Brothers and Graham Brothers Companies. Walter Chrysler couldn't have been very pleased with his new truck-building division, as in each year he owned it, the division's sales had dropped like a rock. By 1932, the truck sales level was almost equal to that of 1918, the first full calendar year Dodge Brothers built commercial vehicles.

Dodge Truck came back with a vengeance in 1933 with the first commercial cars and trucks styled and engineered using a clean sheet of paper by Chrysler Corporation engineers and designers. What didn't change from 1918 was that styling continued to mirror that of corporate automobiles. Dodge commercial vehicle cab and front-end styling was the same as 1933 Dodge passenger cars; trucks even adopted the car's rear-hinged cab doors. Rear-hinged front car doors were a popular item at the time. Commonly called "suicide" doors, they were an idea that was at best marginal for cars and completely out of place with trucks. Less than three years later, this idea was scrapped.

Medium-duty truck styling was the same as that of commercial vehicles, except for a restyled grille, hood, and front fenders to accommodate the heavier truck's larger front wheels and tires and to give them a slightly different appearance than light-duty models. Cabs and

Styling clues to determine a 1937 Dodge commercial vehicle from a 1936 model are subtle. Grille bars in a 1936 commercial vehicle run vertically, while those of a 1937, shown, run horizontally except for the center vertical bars. The ever-popular Dodge double-level commercial panel was then in its fifth production year.

cab interiors of medium-duty trucks were exactly the same as light-duty models.

The division did continue to build 1932 series medium- and heavy-duty models up to and including the eight-cylinder-powered four-ton giants.

Car and light-duty truck styling differed in one important aspect. Because the car business was fashion driven, yearly model changes were expected. Trucks, on the other hand, even while working with the same basic platform as cars, continued for several years without any, or very little, outward styling changes.

At no other time in Dodge Truck history had a truck series been so completely new as these 1933 Dodge H series trucks. Everything about them was new: engines, frames, cabs, suspensions, and so on. We can honestly say these trucks were, "New from the wheels up." Dodge marketing claimed they were, "The Aristocrats of Commercial Cars." One important fundamental of truck styling that had not changed over the years is the belief that good styling is important to buyers because delivery equipment reflects the business, and customers tend to judge a company by what they see, which often is the firm's delivery or service trucks. Dodge trucks were hands-down the beauty winners for 1933. The marketplace was in agreement, causing Dodge truck production to increase by 362 percent to 38,841 units; market share increased by 245 percent.

Dodge Truck's management was not yet ready to make a clean break with the past: new commercial models rode on an automobile's frame instead of a truck frame, as they had since 1918. New commercials were built on either a 111-1/4in wheelbase chassis from the new Dodge DP car series or a 119in wheelbase chassis, which was similar in construction to the shorter version but was not shared with an automobile.

Up to this time, Chrysler Corporation engines were mostly carryovers from either Maxwell or Dodge Brothers.

New Glamour-era half-ton commercial car models did not arrive at dealers until early in 1933. The half-ton pickup was one of the first to be introduced. For 1933 only, the front bumper ends were straight. Over the next two years, Dodge designers tapered bumper ends for a softer appearance. These were the first Dodge trucks engineered and designed by Chrysler from the wheels up.

A tradition that lasted many years began in 1933: the smallest corporate six-cylinder-powered Dodge commercial (half-ton) models. This engine remained in service without major change until 1961, except for adding full-length water jackets for improved cooling in 1935. All four-cylinder engines were dropped from the line at the end of the 1932 models.

New 1933 "Aristocrat" models did not arrive in dealer showrooms until the first of the year, when the commercial series was announced. Commercial models included a pickup, panel, sedan, chassis cowl, and chassis cab. Until new models became available, the company continued to sell unchanged 1932 series trucks.

It was spring 1933 before new one and a half-ton trucks became available. Medium-duty trucks were built on truck-type straight side rail frames with heavy cross-members. Dodge cars' 201ci, 62hp L-head six-cylinder engine was the only engine offered. Standard body offerings included panel, stake, platform, dump, chassis cab with fifth-wheel equipment, and chassis cab.

Two-ton models were introduced immediately after the one and a half-ton. They were powered by the DeSoto's 218ci, 77hp L-head six-cylinder engine. Models offered were stake, platform, dump, chassis cab with fifth-wheel equipment, and chassis cab. Basic truck engines were shared with cars, but truck engines were specifically built for truck service. Every truck engine featured premium components depending upon the severity of the service they were subjected to.

1934 Dodge K Series

With the most important work accomplished in 1933, that of bringing new models to market, 1934 was a year devoted to filling in the gaps in the model lineup and fine-tuning engineering specifications.

One giant leap forward for Dodge Truck was an investment of about $400,000 in new building construction and equipment for an exclusive truck manufacturing plant located in Detroit, entirely segregating truck production from automobile production. This plant built cabs and bodies, painted all sheet metal, contained its own machine shop, plus facilities for fabricating brake drums, brackets, levers, and other items peculiar to trucks, and final assembly lines for frames, chassis, and body mounting. The plant had a 500-units-per-day capacity, including export trucks, in a total floor space of 546,000 square feet (sq-ft).

The commercial car line expanded to include a canopy, screenside, and the new Westchester Suburban wooden-bodied station wagon. Commercial car engineering updates included the more powerful 201ci, 70hp L-head six-cylinder engine. Rear axle ratio

Dodge's wooden-bodied Westchester Suburban station wagon, a new model for 1933, was built on the commercial car's chassis. Several body builders supplied station wagon bodies. The factory shipped a chassis windshield cowl along with running boards, rear fenders, and front seat to the body builder who mounted their body and shipped the completed vehicle to a dealer for customer delivery.

A new model for 1933 was the dual-purpose commercial sedan. It was a two-door sedan with its back windows blanked out and a large sedan delivery-type door cut into the rear of its body. Both steel spoke wheels, shown, and wooden spoke wheels were standard offerings in 1933.

The commercial screenside was a later 1933 model year introduction. Many tradesmen preferred the screen's open body rather than a closed panel body.

Dodge's famous double-level panels built between 1933 and 1938 are fast becoming popular with collectors because of their unique style. A 1934 model is shown. Dodge engineers built a cargo body larger than the cab in order for the body to be large enough to haul practical loads. A passenger car front had a great look, but was too narrow and low for a panel.

was changed to a 4.11:1 to provide faster speeds for delivery service. Front axle was strengthened by changing from the original tubular-type to a truck-type I-beam axle.

More power became available for one and a half-ton and two-ton trucks through the use of larger engines—218ci, 70hp, and 242ci (Chrysler car engine), 85hp, respectively.

1935 Dodge K Series

Dodge Truck's first all-steel cab with front-hinged doors was the major, albeit late, introduction for the year. As far as light-duty models were concerned, only the pickup changed to the new cab. All other models were the cab integral type: canopy, screen, sedan, and panel. These models did not change. Medium-duty and heavy-duty chassis cab models converted to the new cab. The new cab featured an all-steel top; the French-type insert was now history. The only wood pieces left in the cab were in the floorboards.

An interesting new model introduced along with the new cab was a long cargo box pickup. Dodge continued to build a pickup on the 111-1/4in wheelbase chassis, which was 62-3/4in long and became the "short box." Dodge management added a second model, with a 70-3/4in long box built on the 119in wheelbase chassis, which was the "long box" model. These two pickups were an industry first.

On medium- and heavy-duty trucks only, the hood side nameplate was changed from Dodge Brothers to simply Dodge. Light-duty models did not have a nameplate on their hood sides.

Dodge Truck management expanded its manufacturing capabilities by opening a Canadian plant that built 1,500 trucks in 1935; all production was sold in Canada. A second plant was opened in the Los Angeles, California, area to supply the huge Southern California market as well as Northern California, Oregon, Washington, Nevada, and New Mexico. This plant built 5,766 trucks in its first year.

An early 1935 Dodge commercial pickup. Late in the model year, the cab was totally redesigned and given a solid steel roof with front hinged doors. In fact, almost all wood was removed from the cab except for a few floorboards. Note the new steel spoke wheels and fully enclosed spare tire and wheel. Dodge commercial pickups of this era are becoming very popular with collectors. Most collectors paint their pickups in more colorful designs than basic black.

A 1935 Dodge Truck family photo. Left to right: two-ton stake, one and a half-ton stake, commercial panel, and commercial pickup. Note the two stake trucks and pickup have the new cab with front hinged doors. The panel's doors were not changed because its cab was integral with the body. Only the panel has a soft cab roof, and the two medium-duty trucks have hood-side nameplates. Judging by the common paint design, these trucks were intended for promotional purposes.

Dodge's 1936 commercial sedan was a true dual-purpose vehicle. Its cargo area was fully lined in the same manner as a sedan and equipped with a full-width seat, which was easily removed through the large back door in order to convert the car for delivery service. Rear side glass could be blanked out with steel covers. This model was built on the 116in wheelbase passenger-car chassis. It retailed for $755.

The only other new model was a completely re-designed three-ton chassis cab. It continued to be powered by the 310ci big block six-cylinder engine. No body models were offered in the three-ton series, only chassis cabs. The low-volume, eight-cylinder four-ton G-80 heavy-duty series was discontinued.

1936 Dodge L Series

New features of the 1936 Dodge trucks included some of the most significant engineering changes in Dodge Truck's long history. First was the new "Fore-Point," or Balanced Load Distribution. Dodge engineers moved the front axle and wheels 8in rearward so that the front axle carried more of the truck's payload than in the past. Moving the axle back moved the radiator, engine, clutch, transmission, axles, springs, steering gear, and driver's compartment forward of their previous location. Loading space remained the same as before, but infinitely better balance over both front and rear axles was provided. With the new Balanced Load Distribution came a new, more handsome and modern appearance.

The other major engineering breakthrough was a strictly truck-type frame for the half-ton commercial models. Its double drop frame was deeper in siderail cross section and had five truck-type cross-members, including the rear engine support. The commercial sedan was the one exception, as it continued to be a

Engineering-wise, Dodge trucks made a giant leap forward in 1936 with Fore-Point load distribution. Engineers moved the front axle and engine forward, which in turn shifted more of the load's weight to the front axle and wheels. A second advance for light-duty trucks was their new, deep, heavy truck-type frames, which replaced former automobile-type frames. New frames were better suited for carrying heavy loads and easily accepted special bodies.

27

slightly modified Dodge two-door sedan. The commercial sedan was designed to give passenger car riding comfort for the commercial traveler, such as salesmen, while at the same time have carrying capacity for merchandise.

The half-ton truck's wheelbase was stretched to 116in. Now all models were built on one wheelbase in place of two. With the cab moved forward, the frame would accept longer bodies. For example, a half-ton pickup's cargo box length was stretched to 72in from the former 62-3/4in. The new box featured new stake pockets and rolled flareboards. Second, because of moving the front axle forward, the new truck's appearance was more modern. The nation's economy improved for 1936, and Dodge truck sales kept pace, increasing 31

percent, or a total of 109,392 units. Market share increased to 13.4 percent.

1937 Dodge M Series

Management authorized few changes in 1937, as it was only the second year of the Fore-Point era. Appearance-wise, the only exterior change was a new grille and hood side styling. The general shape of the grille remained the same, only the bars within the grille opening varied from vertical to horizontal. Hood side horizontal chrome trim strips were reduced from five strips to three.

Actually, a new instrument panel was a bigger appearance change than new grille and hood details. Dodge designers and engineers introduced a new "High-Safety" dash. High-Safety was a reference to er-

Fore-Point load distribution continued into 1937. Fore-Point resulted in giving Dodge light-duty models a more modern appearance. The new design also allowed designers to extend the length of the half-ton pickup's cargo box for more payload space and weight capacity.

For the first time in 1937, Dodge built three-quarter- and one-ton trucks which were larger versions of half-ton models rather than lighter versions of one and a half-ton trucks. Shown is an MD-21, 136in wheelbase one-ton panel. Drivetrain for the one-ton was the same as half-ton models—218ci, 75hp L-head six and a three-speed truck-type transmission.

gonomic safety issues. All protruding knobs and switches were removed from the dash to prevent injuries as much as possible in the event of a crash or sudden stop. The new design was not only safer but much improved in appearance. A second interior appearance improvement was to simply paint the entire cab interior gray.

The most important mechanical improvement was increased horsepower. After using the 201ci, 70hp six for three years in light-duty trucks, engineers replaced it with the more powerful 218ci, 75hp L-head six.

Dodge truck engineers took an entirely new approach with their three-quarter and one-ton models. Previously, this category had been built down by substituting lighter components such as springs, wheels, and tires on one and a half-ton trucks so they could carry bulky but light loads. For 1937, three-quarter and one-ton trucks were heavier versions of half-ton models. Three-quarter-ton models were built on a 120in wheelbase chassis and one-ton models on a 136in wheelbase chassis. Panel, screen, and canopy were one-ton models only, while pickups, stakes, and platforms were available in either wheelbase length.

This was the first year for a Plymouth pickup. Plymouth pickups were offered as a way of expanding pickup distribution. They were a badge-engineered truck, but with a front styling similar to a Plymouth car and were powered by a smaller engine. The addition of a Plymouth pickup gave DeSoto-Plymouth and Chrysler-Plymouth dealers trucks to sell, which was a great marketing concept. Plymouths were built on the same production line with Dodge pickups. For the first time, all pickups' spare tire carriers were underslung at the rear of the frame.

It wouldn't be a Dodge without a dependable flathead six-cylinder engine. Dodge changed to the bigger 218ci, 75hp engine for all light-duty trucks in 1937 from the previous 201ci, 70hp engine. From 1933 to 1960, the last year for the flathead six, Dodge painted engine blocks aluminum, and engine accessories black.

Previous pages
Dodge's glamorous double-level panel's body ended in what was called a "Beaver Tail." Note how the back of the body slopes down and out at the bottom. This same general shape was repeated in the embossed line pressed into the body sides immediately above the rear fenders. The attractive Dodge commercial panel looked good coming or going.

Total truck production at Chrysler Corporation increased to 121,917 units, but market share fell slightly to 12.9 percent.

1938 Dodge R Series

Dodge Truck was scheduled to move into a new truck factory in time to begin building all new, restyled, and re-engineered 1939 model trucks. The only change of note for 1938 was the change to a new grille style for light-duty trucks. Chrysler designers restyled the truck's grille to bring it into line with the general shape of grilles on all corporate automobiles.

It was a tough year for the nation's economy. After expanding for several years, the economy fell into another deep recession. Industry-wide truck sales were off by more than 50 percent; the same was true for Dodge truck sales.

Even though Chrysler had owned the company for nine years, Dodge Truck continued to display the Dodge Brothers name and logo on an attractive winged medallion fastened to the center of the commercial truck's grille.

Chrysler Corporation chose the Rocky Mountain, or Bighorn, ram for its Dodge car symbol in 1932 and truck symbol in 1933. It was thought that the fearless and sure-footed ram's image was in keeping with the power and dependability that had brought fame to Dodge cars and trucks.

The last year for this series was 1938. The only change was a new grille style, patterned after the grilles on all corporate automobiles. The special-bodied one-ton Detroit Police Depart-ment vans featured high-style chrome-plated grilles and radiator shells.

Chapter 3

Collectors' Favorites
1939–1947

Dodge called its new 1939 models, "The truck of the year." They were built in a giant new truck plant that had been designed by the outstanding industrial architect Albert Kahn. The plant was the most modern facility in the world for building trucks. Sitting on 48.94 acres of land, the plant's floor space totaled 658,000sq-ft. Its two assembly lines stretched 1,260ft (nearly a quarter of a mile) and could turn out Dodge trucks at a rate that surpassed any other truck plant in the United States. All areas of the building received natural light from 150,000sq-ft of glass. Dodge management believed its work force could build a better product if they had the advantage of light, airy, and agreeable working conditions. The plant went into operation on October 10, 1938.

1939 Dodge T Series
The new 1939 Dodge truck would prove to be a design classic. It served Dodge, with only a few minor changes, until 1948. Highlights of the design included horizontal grille work, which curved into a wide chrome-plated vertical bar in the center of the grille, joined by chrome moldings that swept down and in from each side. Louvers extended across a wide raised apron to the massive fenders, giving a lower, heavier appearance to the front end.

Deeply crowned front fenders had a wide apron at the rear which hid the undercarriage. Four speed-line ridges at the rear bottom of the front fenders added a suggestion of movement. Teardrop-shaped

WC series (TC in 1939 and VC in 1940, but WC from 1941 on) half-ton pickups dating from 1939 to 1947 are the hands-down favorite trucks owned by Dodge collectors. This 1940 low-mileage, unrestored, original-condition VC pickup is the best of the best. Power was provided by a 201ci, 79hp flathead six-cylinder engine.

headlight buckets mounted high on the inside of the crowned front fenders contributed to better night vision. A stylized flying Dodge Ram ornament perched atop the hood.

The new cab featured a sloping V-type, two-piece windshield that could be cranked open for ventilation. A cowl top ventilator provided additional ventilation. Door windows were not equipped with vent wings.

The cab's roof lines were smooth and rounded. Due to new splash shields below the doors, the smooth, clean lines extended down to the running boards.

Dodge called the new instrument cluster a High-Safety panel because all control buttons were recessed and all gauges were located directly in front of the driver. A large glovebox, which Dodge called a dispatch compartment, was positioned to the right of the instruments. As was typical on trucks until the 1960s, both doors locked from the inside, but only the right door could be locked from the outside.

While the body was completely restyled for 1939, engines were unchanged from the previous year. In fact, the family of L-head sixes used in the Dodge truck line was now six years old. The only new engine in Dodge's line was a 331ci diesel, which went into production on October 22, 1938.

Two engines powered Dodge's light-duty line: a 201ci L-6 in half-ton models and a 218ci L-6 in three-quarter and one-ton models.

The half-ton pickup was an exceptionally fine-looking truck. Rear fenders were full-skirted, smooth, and rounded, following the lines of the new front fenders. The lower rear fender skirts, like the front fender skirts, also featured four speed-line ridges. The pickup box measured 6-1/2ft long, 4ft wide, and 17in deep. The bed floor was constructed of 13/16in thick oak boards with steel skid strips. Prior to 1939, Dodge pickup floors had been constructed of steel.

Gone was the uniquely styled Dodge double-level panel. The new panel carried smart, modern lines, though the center of the roof was still covered with weatherproof fabric. Double doors opened at the rear for easy loading. The cargo floor's construction was oak boards covered with steel skid strips. A rear bumper was standard equipment. Panels also shared with pickups the same full-length running boards and rear fenders. The driver's seat was the individual bucket type. A second seat was optional. Inside, load space length measured a generous 92in long.

Canopy and screen models differed from each other only in that the screen model was equipped with wire

Right
A 1940 half-ton pickup's cargo box was 6-1/2ft long. The box interior width was 48-1/4in, wide enough to carry standard 4ft-wide building material flat on the floor. The floor in the cargo box was constructed of oak boards covered with steel skid strips. Half-ton pickups rode on a 116in wheelbase chassis and were rated for a 1,000lb payload.

Dodge's 1939 model trucks were all new and built in the new state-of-the-art truck assembly plant located in Warren, Michigan, a Detroit suburb. The 133in wheelbase TD, one-ton pickup with 9ft cargo box was new in 1939. Collectors generally prefer half-ton pickups, but these big one-tonners are available for anyone interested.

Beginning in 1939 and continuing through 1947, Dodge set a pattern of building both 116in wheelbase half-ton and 133in wheelbase one-ton pickups, panels, canopies, and screens.

Available three-quarter-ton 120in models included a pickup and stake. One-ton 120in wheelbase pickups and stakes were also offered. Here are three 1939 133in wheelbase one-ton panels.

Parking lights were moved to the top of the headlight shells in 1940 with the changeover to sealed-beam headlights. Beginning in 1941, Dodge designers moved the headlights outboard to the crown of the front fenders to better mark the total width of the truck for oncoming traffic.

to completely enclose the driver's compartment was available as an extra-cost option.

Dodge Truck's standard scheme was to paint fenders, running boards, and the lower radiator grille black. The upper grille, radiator shell, and hood were painted cab color. Bumpers were painted aluminum. Dodge truck standard paint colors were light blue, yellow, dark blue, green, gray, red, and black.

Dodge built 83,660 trucks in calendar year 1939, which was a whopping 68.2 percent gain over 1938's production. Dodge plants in Canada turned out 5,704 trucks in 1939, a 47 percent gain over 1938. Trucks were assembled at the new main truck plant in Warren, Michigan, and in Los Angeles and Canada.

Dodge built a full line of trucks in 1939, ranging in size from half-ton to three-ton, including three diesel-powered models. As was the custom of the time, in the light-duty line Dodge made Miser models available, which were equipped with a smaller 1in carburetor. A throttle-stop, or governor, was available for all models.

1940 Dodge V Series

Dodge designers took an attractive truck that was new the year before and improved it for 1940. Appearance changes were limited to the front end. The 1939 models featured a V-shaped chromed design element which was positioned low on the grille and swept up to the right and left. This design detail was weak in appearance.

Dodge designers made a substantial improvement to the front end appearance of 1940 models by replacing the original chrome pieces with new chrome trim that flowed back to the left and right over the catwalks. The new chrome-plated V-shaped section was placed higher and had louvers matching those that extended across the wide raised apron to the fenders on either side. A wide chrome bar, which ran from one side of the grille to the other, carried the Dodge name in its center on a red-painted background. The new front-end design gave Dodge trucks a heavier, more massive look.

Other improvements included new sealed-beam headlights on all models except three-ton trucks. A small parking light was placed on top of the headlight housing. To supply the current for the new 50-candle-power lights, 1940 models were equipped with a 35-amp generator.

Another new feature, which would become a Dodge trademark for years to come, was wheel mounting bolts and lug nuts with right- and left-hand threads to prevent loosening.

Series designation was changed to V from T in 1939. Brake horsepower for the half-ton VC model was

screen over the open sides to protect the load. Canopy models were a cross between a panel and a pickup. The body was constructed with pickup box-type sides including flareboards and a tailgate; the floor was made of 13/16in thick oak with skid strips. A top constructed of wood longitudinal strips ran from the windshield header to the rear-most part of the body. The wood frame was covered with weatherproof fabric. Heavy black canvas roll-up curtains covered the open sides and back. One bucket seat was standard, and rear bumpers were optional on canopy and screen models. A partition

Right
Dodge's 1946 one-ton WD-21, 133in wheelbase stake truck was unchanged in style from prewar trucks. Note the headlight's location on the crown of the front fenders in comparison to the headlight location on the 1940 pickup. Stake body was a factory-installed item.

increased from 70 at 3000rpm to 79 at 3000rpm, and the maximum torque increased from 148lb-ft at 1200rpm to 154lb-ft at 1200rpm. Maximum GVW increased from 4,000lb to 4,200lb.

Maximum GVW for the three-quarter-ton VD-15 model was increased from 6,000 to 6,400lb. Brake horsepower increased from 77 to 82 at 3000rpm, and maximum engine torque was increased from 158 to 166lb-ft at 1200rpm. A new hypoid-type rear axle with a new barrel-type differential permitted the use of larger and stronger differential gears. Standard paint colors carried over with no additions or deletions from 1939.

Only one new model was announced for 1940. This was the first-ever Dodge-built cab-over-engine, a one and a half-ton truck in three wheelbase lengths: 105in, 129in, and 159in. Dodge called it the Road-Pilot due to the superior visibility it afforded the driver.

Sales for calendar year 1940 ran 13 percent ahead of 1939, topping at 54,323. Total industry sales amounted to 559,150, or 14.9 percent ahead of 1939. Total Dodge truck production for the United States and Canada for calendar year 1940 was 117,588. Of this total, 104,938 were built in Michigan, 4,860 in Los Angeles, and 7,790 in Canada.

Government sales jumped ahead considerably in 1940 as the armed forces stepped up their buying in preparation for World War II.

This was the first year Dodge Truck used its famous Job-Rated advertising theme. The Job-Rated concept was quite simple:
· A truck that was too small for a job or too large for a job was costly, so Dodge built 112 standard chassis and body models—one to fit every job.
· Trucks that were underpowered or overpowered were wasteful. Dodge built six different truck engines so the buyer could select the correct engine for a desired model.
· Trucks correctly sized and powered for their jobs last longer. Any Dodge truck could be ordered with a variety of clutches, transmissions, and rear axles.

1941 Dodge W Series

Appearance changes to the 1941 Dodge trucks were minimal. For a more balanced frontal appearance,

The W series trucks' instrument panel remained essentially unchanged from 1939 to 1947. A new air-controlled seat cushion was easily adjusted to suit the driver's weight and road condition.

The Dodge trucks' grille was redesigned in 1941; the new design remained unchanged through 1947. It has become an American classic.

Dodge engineers continued to prefer the butterfly-type hood until 1957. It allowed the rear of the engine to be as easily accessed as the front of the engine.

headlights were moved to the center of the front fenders where they were mounted in pockets formed into the fenders. Parking lights moved to the cowl and changed to a bullet-shaped design. The hood ornament was changed to a stylized version of the original Flying Ram. These appearance changes would be the last made to this body style, which was now in its third model year.

New two-tone paint designs were offered at no extra charge in 1941. Cab and hood could be painted one of the seven standard colors, with fenders and lower part of the radiator grille in the buyer's choice of any of the other colors. The customer could also have his truck painted one solid color without charge. Previously, fenders and running boards were painted black regardless of cab color.

A deluxe cab equipment package was also new for 1941. The deluxe package consisted of genuine brown leather upholstery on the seat cushion and back, air foam seat cushion and back cushion construction, armrest on left door, a single electric windshield wiper in place of the standard vacuum type, dome light, one interior sun visor, and a chrome windshield frame. This deluxe package was available on any Dodge truck for an extra charge of $25; no charge for diesel models, which offered this equipment as standard.

The only new model for 1941 was a two-ton cab-over-engine available in 105in, 129in, and 159in wheelbase lengths. The two-ton COE was powered by the big-block L-6 engine of 242ci, developing 99hp at 3000rpm.

Dodge built a complete line of Job-Rated trucks in 1941 from half- to three-tons. Six different engines were used including a diesel. There were seventeen rear axle ratios, twenty-three frames, four clutches, six brake

Dodge changed the front style, as seen here on a 1947 half-ton canopy, in 1941. Except for a few engineering improvements, postwar Dodge trucks were essentially the same as 1942 mod- els. This was the last year Dodge built either a canopy or screen model.

combinations, ten basic spring combinations, and eight rear axles in the line.

Dodge Truck enjoyed a good year during calendar year 1941. Sales of 62,925 were up 15.9 percent over 1940. Industry sales of 640,697 were up 14.6 percent. Production for all of North America peaked at 166,602. It was Dodge's best year ever with production 41.7 percent ahead of 1940. Of this total, 7,164 units were built in Canada and 147,062 in Warren, Michigan.

Government sales became more important than ever as World War II drew closer.

1942 Dodge W Series

In an effort to improve performance and to bring power outputs into line with major competitors—Ford and Chevrolet—Dodge revamped its light-duty engines for 1942. All half-ton models were given the 218ci L-6 engine. This was the same engine as had been used in three-quarter and one-ton models since 1939. All three-quarter-ton models continued to use the 218ci, but one-ton models now used the 230ci L-6 engine. Maximum output of the 218 was 95hp at 3600rpm, while torque was 172lb-ft at 1200rpm. Compression ratio was

6.8:1. Maximum horsepower of the 230 was 105 at 3600rpm, and torque was 184lb-ft at 1200rpm. Compression ratio for the 230 was 6.8:1.

Total calendar year production for 1942 was the largest in Dodge history, totaling 169,837. Production for all of North America breaks down as follows: Michigan, 125,752; Los Angeles, 2,420; and Canada, 41,665.

Production of passenger cars and trucks for civilian use was discontinued January 31, 1942.

1946 Dodge W Series

No appearance changes were made to the 1946 Dodge truck line. Several new mechanical features were added as a result of experience gained in building military

Right
Dodge advertising described its 1947 one and a half-ton cab-over-engine models as, "High, Wide and Handsome!" Who could argue with this claim? Here is a 1947 Dodge WFM one and a half-ton, 105in wheelbase cab-over-engine chassis cab with fifth-wheel equipment. Dodge built its first cab-over-engine model in 1940. Dodge offered two series in 1947: one and a half-ton and two-ton models.

This grille design was unique to cab-over-engine trucks. The stylized hood ornament was the same as that of all other 1947 model trucks, however.

Dodge's cab-over-engine was unique in that it retained full-width doors and a full-width seat. The driver could quickly and easily "walk up" and into the cab assisted by three steps: running board, a convenient step pad, and cab floor. The instrument panel was the same as the standard cab's. The transmission's shift lever is connected to the rear-mounted transmission via a reach rod.

trucks. A new oil pump provided maximum oil pressure at low engine speeds, even while idling. Rear axle housing vents on all models opened to relieve pressure built up in the differential. This provided a more positive seal against dirt. Heavier steering gears on all models provided longer life and greater steering ease. In half-ton models, steering adjustment was made easier and the steering ratio was increased. Universal joints were made heavier in all models. The half-ton and one-ton models were given a new four-pinion-type differential to replace the former two-pinion-type unit. The seat cushion and back were redesigned for greater driver comfort, and the seat cushions were equipped with a manually operated air control valve by which drivers could regulate the amount of air in the cushion according to their weight. Seat and back spring construction was new as well, and they were covered with an improved vinyl upholstery material.

Total sales for calendar year 1946 were 94,490, a 53.3 percent increase over 1941 and a solid third place in U.S. truck sales. Total calendar year production amounted to 144,968, with 122,298 built in Detroit, 9,751 in Los Angeles, and 12,919 in Canada.

1947 Dodge W Series

In this, the final year of the W series trucks, Dodge invested all of its resources in the development of an all-new completely re-engineered and restyled line of trucks to be introduced the following year. Subsequently, no appearance or engineering changes were made.

Payload and GVWs on half-ton and three-quarter-ton models were increased through the addition of higher-capacity front axles. No models were added or dropped, and all other specifications remained the same.

Dodge set records for both sales and production in calendar year 1947. Its sales of 126,736 represented a 31.3 percent increase over the previous year, and its total production of 183,953 for all of North America represented a 26.9 percent increase. Production in Michigan was 153,255, Los Angeles was 13,320, and Canada was 17,378.

Chapter 4

Tough Military and Power Wagons 1939–1968

To understand the Power Wagon requires us to take a big step backward in Dodge history. (See Chapter One for additional background on Dodge's military history.)

In 1914, the Dodge brothers began building a car which they positioned a little above Henry Ford's Model T in terms of power, size, and price. The Dodge car was an immediate success due to its exceptional quality and value. In those early years, Dodge Brothers sold all the cars they could build. Consequently, they had no interest in building a commercial vehicle. In 1917, however, two outside forces finally convinced them to begin building commercials. One was their dealers who kept insisting they needed a commercial to satisfy customer demands; the other was the U.S. Army. Because of Dodge Brothers' excellent reputation for dependability (a word coined to describe Dodge quality), the Army contracted with Dodge Brothers to build an ambulance and a light repair truck. The light repair truck looked like a pickup with a canvas top.

In the fall of 1917, a few months before the introduction of the first civilian vehicle, Dodge Brothers had already shipped thousands of these trucks for use in World War I. Dodge Brothers' first commercial car, the screenside, was actually a civilian version of its military screenside.

In 1946, this bit of Dodge history repeated itself. During World War II, Dodge was the Army's prime contractor for three-quarter-ton four-wheel-drive trucks. Dodge built its first Army four-wheel-drive in 1934, but large scale production didn't begin until 1939 when a half-ton four-wheel-drive was developed based on a conventional civilian half-ton truck. A year later, a second half-ton series was developed featuring military-type sheet metal. Severe testing proved the half-ton couldn't stand up to the rigorous duty the Army had in mind for its lightest four-wheel-drive truck. Dodge engineers responded by developing the heavier three-quarter-ton four-wheel-drive truck, which was mass-produced for World War II. This truck was lower, wider, and more powerful.

Dodge brought the Power Wagon to market in 1946 for the same reason it introduced the screenside in 1917: it saw an unfilled market niche and had a vehicle to fill it. Besides, the tooling and start-up costs had already been paid for by the government. The 1950 Dodge truck sales manual makes the point: "The Dodge Power Wagon . . . is without competition. No other truck manufacturer offers a model that is at all comparable. The Dodge Power Wagon was designed and built to meet a definite need. It's a vehicle built for continuous operation under extreme conditions. Its four-wheel-drive gives it tractive ability for off-the-road service that would stall an ordinary truck . . . takes it places you wouldn't expect any truck to go."

The sales manual proceeded to list seventy-five types of businesses, ranging from airports to well-drillers, that could be prospects for a Power Wagon. Consider also that the production tooling and engineering development costs for the Power Wagon's mechanical components had already been paid for by the U.S. government from the 255,196 military vehicles the Army purchased during World War II. Dodge had a product that did not require volume production in order to make a profit. The 1946 Power Wagon sales catalog proclaimed on the front cover that this is, "The Army truck the boys wrote home about . . . now redesigned for peacetime use."

Power Wagon says Dodge tough and dependability better than any other truck built by Dodge in its long history. The rock-solid, one-ton four-wheel-drive pickup was only in its second year of production when this beautiful 1947 brute was built. Dodge built this truck "to take it." It is a real "Power Wagon," the truck that "doesn't need roads."

Dodge supplied more than 5,000 trucks to the Army in 1935; some were four-wheel drives, but most were two-wheel drives such as this pickup. The Army purchased three half-ton commercial models: pickup, panel, and Westchester Suburban sta- tion wagon. All three trucks were essentially civilian trucks, except for a heavy-duty grille guard, steel channel front bumper, and tow hooks.

Dodge was one of the Army's leading truck suppliers during World War I. Shown is a general-cargo truck. Dodge built only the chassis and open cab; the pickup-like body and canvas cover were built by an outside supplier. These trucks served with the U.S. Army in France.

Let's take a look at that "redesigned for peacetime use" truck. Power Wagon's cab dated from 1939's T series (which was still in production when the Power Wagon first appeared in 1946), yet looked like an Army design. The grille, made from solid round steel bars, and the radiator, with its external cap, were very much Army design, as was the front bumper and winch mechanism. Keeping another military-styling touch, designers chose a simple, rugged splash-guard look for the front fenders. Running boards, rear fenders, and pickup box were basically civilian issue. A factory rear bumper was not available. Bullet-shaped headlights perched on top of the forward curve of the fender were the same as on Dodge's conventional trucks. And, of course, the tires were the deep-cleated military type. Power Wagons sat quite tall due to large wheels and tires and the fact that it was four-wheel-drive, but nevertheless, the front axle and differential were tucked up below the truck and were not in full view.

Dodge constantly emphasized that the Power Wagon was unique due to its four-wheel-drive capability. Equally emphasized was its ruggedness, which

Dodge's first production four-wheel-drive military vehicles for World War II consisted of the 1940 VC series with civilian sheet metal. Dodge built six body versions in the VC series; the VC-1 Command Reconnaissance, shown, was used by field commanders. Dodge built more of this model than any other truck in the series.

The second series WC half-ton four-wheel-drive Army trucks were built in 1941–1942. WC series trucks featured military-type front sheet metal, a slightly larger engine and rear axle, and some had front-mounted power winches. More open-cab Weapons Carriers, shown, were built than any other model. A canvas top covering both cab and body was provided for this truck.

Production on the final model Dodge four-wheel-drive World War II Army truck began in April 1942. These three-quarter-ton capacity trucks were wider and lower than the preceding half-ton trucks and featured high-flotation tires and heavier-duty components than the first two half-ton series. Shown from left are a WC-6 Command Reconnaissance without winch, a 1941 half-ton with military sheet metal, and a 1940 half-ton with civilian sheet metal. Dodge built more than 255,000 three-quarter-ton four-wheel-drive trucks for World War II.

Dodge converted its three-quarter-ton four-wheel-drive military truck for civilian service by redesigning its front end and adding a pickup cargo box and a conventional truck cab. All mechanical components were essentially unchanged from the military version. This 1945 engineering prototype with civilian one-ton pickup cargo box was initially called a "Farm Utility" truck. A name which thankfully was later changed to Power Wagon.

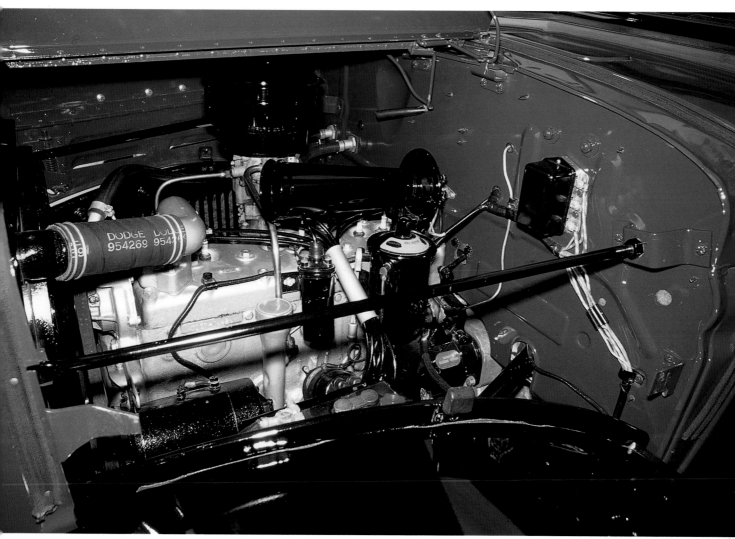

This Power Wagon's engine has been meticulously restored to new condition, as has the rest of the truck. Standard engine for the WDX one-ton Power Wagon was the 230ci, 94hp L-head six cylinder. Transmission is a four-speed with two power take-off openings; one goes forward to the winch, and the second goes to the rear tail shaft.

made the Power Wagon as at home off-road as on-road. Dodge marketed the Power Wagon on these three premises: the customer could use it for pulling power, in place of a tractor pulling a plow; for portable power, as in running a saw; or for carrying power, as in a truck hauling a load. The salesman's challenge was to convince customers to create jobs for the Power Wagon to handle. The sales literature urged, "Its usefulness is restricted only by the ingenuity of the owner!"

For pulling, a drawbar, which was adjustable for height and off-center towing, was available as an extra-cost option. Also, a heavy-duty pintle hook could be mounted on the frame cross-member. By using these two towing devices, a customer could find many jobs for the Power Wagon to handle.

Beginning in 1949, the Monroe Auto Equipment Company of Monroe, Michigan, manufactured a hy-

draulic lift kit and a complete line of farming and road building accessories for the Power Wagon. The lift kit consisted of a hydraulic pump and valve unit that mounted on the front of the engine, a three-point implement hitch located at the rear, and a control lever installed inside the cab. Available implements included a plow, cultivator, rotary hoe, terracing blade, harrow, hydrograder, land leveler, lift-type scoop, earth mover, buzz saw, post-hole digger, springtooth harrow, and double disc harrow. Dodge advertised that the Power Wagon could easily pull a three-bottom 14in plow and encouraged farmers to use the Power Wagon in place of a tractor.

Dodge was not alone in competing for the farm tractor business during the early postwar period. Jeep promoted a similar implement line, and even Crosley marketed its little Jeep-like Farm-O-Road to compete for the small farm market. Although the farm was the

location most often pictured to demonstrate the pulling ability of the Power Wagon, there were many other jobs that Dodge salesmen could target. Power Wagon's uniqueness probably was most apparent in its portable power application. Several special features enabled Power Wagon to serve as a portable power source. All Power Wagons had power take-offs on both sides of their transmissions. The forward shaft transmitted power to the winch, while the other transferred power rearward through the tailshaft.

The power take-off operated at 61-1/2 percent of engine speed when rotating in the direction of engine rotation and 47-1/2 percent of engine speed when rotating the opposite direction. Engagement and direction of rotation were controlled by a single lever inside the cab. The tailshaft could be used to power a pulley drive that mounted on a pillow block at the center of the frame's rear cross-member. The pulley measured 9in in diameter by 6-5/8in wide and could be governed at SASE standard belt speed of 3,100ft per minute. The Power Wagon was an ideal power source for a variety of stationary power jobs. A common one was with public utilities to bore holes and set poles.

In addition, a mechanical governor attached to the engine was offered as an extra-cost option to set the engine speed of any auxiliary equipment powered by the tailshaft or pulley drive. The governor could also limit engine speed during over-the-road operation. The governor was belt-driven from the water pump shaft and was controlled by a speed setting inside the cab.

Dodge engineers fitted the Power Wagon with special features to assure proper cooling when the truck was being driven slowly or while operating stationary equipment. These cooling devices included a six-blade 18in diameter fan, a partial fan shroud, and a 3in thick (1/2in thicker than normal) radiator. A radiator overflow tank was also offered as extra-cost equipment.

In terms of carrying power, the Power Wagon was a brute. Its pickup box, measuring 96-1/16in long by 54in wide by 22-1/4in high, with a capacity of 58 cubic feet (cu-ft), was of generous size. The Power Wagon's floor was covered with oak planks and steel skid strips. Stake pockets would accommodate two-by-four stakes. Power Wagon's maximum GVW ratings were 7,600lb and 8,700lb, and from 1957 on, 9,500lb. The heavier GVW ratings were achieved by adding extra-cost 1,600lb capacity front springs, 3,000lb capacity rear main springs, and larger tires.

Standard tire size for 7,600lb maximum GVW rating was 7.50x8PR. For 8,700lb maximum GVW rating,

the extra-cost tires were 9.00x8PR, and in 1957 the GVW included 9.00x10PR tires. All tires were on 16in wheels; the same tire was used front and rear.

Dodge engineers improved Power Wagon's pickup box in 1952. The original box had used smooth sheet metal sides and stake pockets. The redesign used three stake pockets and the sides were ribbed for strength and improved styling. The new cargo box was the same style used on conventional Dodge pickups, although

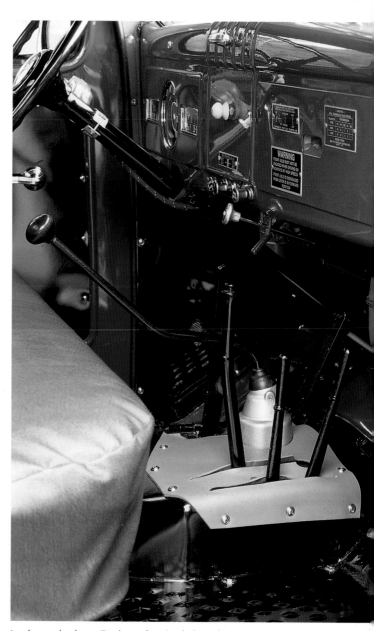

In the early days, Dodge advertised that the Power Wagon could accommodate three adults comfortably on its wide, deeply cushioned seat. The seat may have been wide enough for three adults, but where would the center person put his or her feet? Directly in front of the center person are the gear shift lever, emergency brake lever, a lever for four-wheel-drive, and a lever for high- and low-speed four-wheel-drive ranges.

Power Wagon was designed to be the champion "load-lugger" of the light-duty truck field. Maximum GVW rating was a big 8,700lb. Dodge engineers designed an oversized cargo box to accommodate the loads it was built to haul. Its cargo box measured slightly over 8ft long, 54in wide, and 22-1/4in deep. Four stake pockets on each side were big enough to accept stakes made from two-by-fours.

only the 8ft pickup box was used on the Power Wagon. Cab and chassis versions were also sold for mounting bodies for specialized needs. Many Power Wagons were also fitted with 9ft stake bodies.

Dodge used the dependable 230ci, 94hp L-head six-cylinder engine in the Power Wagon from 1946 to 1960. This engine remained essentially unchanged over its life. By 1960, its gross horsepower was boosted to 113 and gross torque was up to 198lb-ft. The 251ci, 125hp L-head engine that replaced it in 1961 was another dependable Dodge L-head truck engine with many years of service in one and a half- and two-ton trucks. The 251 engine's block was larger, longer, and entirely different from that of the 230.

Power Wagon's four-speed transmission was extra rugged with carburized gears. It had power take-off openings on both sides, a two-speed transfer case located directly behind the transmission, and a 1:1 ratio in

Left
Most Power Wagons produced were pickups, but Dodge did supply many chassis cab or chassis cowl models, shown, on which special bodies such as this 1950 school bus were mounted.

This 1962 Dodge W100 half-ton Town Wagon Power Wagon could get work crews and their equipment to off-road job sites with complete protection from the weather. Two rear seats could be removed to haul bulky loads; full-width-opening rear doors provided easy access to the cargo area. Power Wagons offered six-cylinder and V-8 engines, three-speed or four-speed manual transmissions, and six- or eight-passenger seating. *Chrysler Corporation*

Because of their off-road ability, Power Wagon fire trucks were well suited for fighting brushfires. Here is a 1960 W200 three-quarter-ton Power Wagon with dual rear wheels. This is an interesting truck because Dodge did not build a three-quarter-ton truck with dual rear wheels as a standard model. This truck was engineered and built by the Special Equipment Group. Dual rear wheels allowed it to carry enough water to effectively fight brushfires far from water sources. Fire equipment and body were from American LaFrance. *Chrysler Corporation.*

Functional purposes for the M37B1 Weapons Carrier included troop transportation on fold-up wooden benches, transporting weapons and ammunition, radio truck, and countless other miscellaneous tasks. Rolled-up canvas could be lowered to enclose both sides and rear.

Left
Dodge's three-quarter-ton four-wheel-drive M37B1 military truck series dates from 1958. This series was built on and off through 1968. A 1963 M37B1, a Vietnam-era vehicle, is shown. M37B1s differed from M37s, the Korean War version, by the following improvements: new electrical connectors, cable harnessing, magnetic drain plugs, brake cylinder cups, reflectors, and revised canvas top. The truck shown is fitted with "snorkel" gear for fording.

high and a 1.96:1 ratio in low. With the transfer case in low range, the transmission in first gear, and a 5.83:1 rear axle ratio, the overall drive ratio was 73.1:1. With front-wheel-drive disengaged, only the 1:1 transfer case ratio could be used.

Like everything else, the frame of the Power Wagon was built extra heavy and rugged for severe off-road service. The frame had seven cross-members and inside channel siderail reinforcements.

The Power Wagon remained basically unchanged for the entire twenty-two years it was on the market. By 1968, this almost thirty-year-old truck cab, which originated in 1939, was an anachronism. But where else could a truck buyer with a specialized need purchase such a rugged dependable unit?

Power Wagon sales for the domestic market ceased in 1968 but continued for export sales and MDAP (Military Defense Assistance Program) until 1978. Late in life, the 225 slant six replaced the 251ci L-head six. Power Wagons built for MDAP were usually a chassis cab without a top to which a variety of bodies could be mounted, typically, either ambulances or command cars.

Left
Cab interior is complete down to a weapon's rack loaded with the correct weapons.

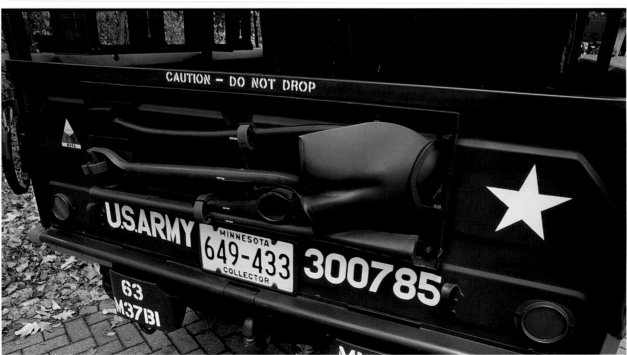

Not an inch of space was unused. The outside of the tailgate was the logical place to store an ax, pick ax, and shovel where they could be instantly removed when needed.

Throughout its entire production life, the M37 and M37B1 engine was the basic Dodge 230ci L-head six from World War II fame. M37B1, however, was equipped with an upgraded 24-volt electrical system.

Chapter 5

Practical Pickups and Power Giant V-8 Trucks 1948–1960

In December 1947, Dodge launched its first all-new truck since 1939. Dodge followed Chevrolet and GMC (June 1947 and July 1947, respectively), and was one month ahead of Ford's January 1948 introduction.

Dodge advertising for the B series featured two themes: first, Pilot-House safety cabs was an all-new theme; and the second, Job-Rated, had been the central theme in Dodge truck advertising since 1940.

In January 1948, when Ford introduced its all-new truck line, it also introduced an interesting new concept—identifying trucks by size. Ford did this by attaching a nameplate to each cowl. The nameplate numbered the size of the truck from F-1 for half-ton up to F-8 for three-ton. The concept was so popular that Chevrolet picked it up the following year, and subsequently, all truck manufacturers adopted the practice, except Dodge. It would be another nine years before Dodge followed suit.

According to Dodge, eight basic sizes would not adequately fit a truck to a specific job. A truck too small for the job would not perform properly, and a truck too

Dodge Truck's 1948 to 1953 models can be termed B series, Practical pickups, or Pilot-House pickups. The 1948 and 1949 models do not have any visible differences in appearance or engineering. Dodge considered them the same series. Shown is a model B-1-B-108. The first letter stands for the entire series 1948 to 1953; the number one denotes 1948 and 1949 model years; B is for half-ton; and 108 is its wheelbase length in inches. "Practical" refers to its deep cargo box; these trucks were designed and built for carrying big loads. Practical also refers to their simple cycle-type rear fenders, which could be quickly and easily unbolted and replaced in case of damage. "Pilot-House" is a reference to its expanded glass area over the former W series trucks. Windows are wider and higher, plus rear cab quarter windows were added as an option. In addition, the driver sat higher on chair-height seats for maximum visibility.

large for the job meant the customer paid for more truck than was required. In 1948, Dodge offered a total of 248 basic models. In the next few years the total would grow to 356. With 248 basic chassis models in the line, Dodge assumed it could satisfy more than 97 percent of all hauling needs.

Basic mechanical components of the B series did not vary from those of the preceding W series, and all other mechanical components—including clutches, transmissions, rear axles, and two light-duty engines—carried over unchanged. The major engineering advancements of the B series involved wheelbase lengths and steering components.

To achieve better weight distribution, Dodge engineers moved the engine forward and the front axle back. More weight now rested on the front wheels. This was a wise move because the front wheels normally carry a small percentage of the total body and payload weight. By increasing the weight carried on the front wheels, payloads increased without increasing the load on the rear wheels and axle.

Another important feature of the B series was its amazing maneuverability. This feature gave Dodge a tremendous advantage over the competition. Better maneuverability resulted from shorter wheelbase lengths. Moving the front axle backward shortened the wheelbase by approximately 8in.

An exceptionally wide front tread permitted turning the wheels at a sharper angle to allow for smaller turning circles and better maneuverability. It also provided greater stability, which was an important safety factor.

Another major factor that contributed to exceptional maneuverability was cross-steering. In combination with a wide-tread front axle, cross-steering provided a 37deg turning angle. Typically, competitive trucks, with their inferior steering design, had larger turning diameters to the left because the left front tire interfered with the drag link. With cross-steering, the drag link ran almost parallel with the front axle and did not interfere with the left front tire when turning.

Shorter wheelbases, however, did not affect the all-important CA (back of cab to rear axle) dimensions. Purchasers of new Dodge trucks could easily mount the bodies from their old trucks onto their new Dodges.

In preparing the design criteria for the B series cabs, Dodge engineers put driver comfort first. Their research showed that a comfortable driver is safer, more efficient, and most important, more productive.

Shortened wheelbases and cross-steering resulted in ease of handling. In addition to easy handling, the B series featured long flexible springs and shock absorbers to provide a comfortable, controlled ride. The

cab design also provided maximum roominess, comfort, convenience, and safety.

Dodge engineers designed a cab with an abundance of headroom, legroom, and seats wide enough for three husky men. Chair-high seats provided a natural, comfortable seating position. The seat adjusted to meet the requirements of each driver. Another exclusive Dodge feature was an Air-O-Ride seat cushion. The amount of air within the cushion could be adjusted by a lever located at the front bottom of the cushion to make a firmer or softer ride.

Doors extended below the cab floor and were sealed by sponge rubber weather seals to aid in keeping drafts out. Dodge went to considerable lengths to provide all-weather cab ventilation. For warm weather

A rear view of this Practical pickup reveals how deep its cargo box is; note the box is nearly as high as the cab's belt line. The rear bumper was an extra-cost option and is not often seen. This truck is a low-mileage, unrestored, like-new truck.

Dodge was the first of the Big Three to design a pickup whose front fenders were integral and cab-wide, a Dodge Truck design innovation that gives these trucks a more advanced-design appearance.

driving, the cowl ventilator scooped in generous quantities of cool air. Standard equipment on DeLuxe and Custom cabs, ventilating wings operated on friction-type points, without the use of crank-type regulators. Finally, door windows operated by regulators to provide additional air when needed. Divider posts on cabs equipped with ventilating wings moved down with the door windows. This was an advantage over fixed-type divider posts, because an obstruction in the window opening was eliminated, allowing the driver to make hand signals more easily.

One of the most important features of the new cab was Pilot-House vision. Drivers enjoyed clear vision in all directions: up high to see traffic lights, down over the hood, and to each side through the new high wide windshield. With the chair-height seat and a flat steering wheel angle, the driver looked over the steering wheel instead of through it. With rear quarter windows, the driver had clear vision on every side, a definite safety improvement.

Another outstanding feature of Dodge cabs was their handsome interiors. Cabs were fully trimmed with a rich grained imitation leather that combined attractiveness with great durability. Door panels, headliner, cowl kick panels, and firewall were all covered in leather-look trim to give a comfortable feel instead of the cold feeling of steel panels.

Concern with driver ergonomics motivated Dodge engineers in 1948. Driver comfort extended to easily read instruments and to convenient controls. Instruments grouped in front of the driver could readily be seen, and by using large white numerals on black backgrounds, all instruments could be easily read. In addition, indirect lighting provided good visibility for night driving.

To facilitate servicing, instruments could be removed through the front of the instrument panel. Wiring and connections could be installed in the open, without the need to work behind the instrument panel.

Buyers had their choice of three cab trim options:
· Standard cab: sun visor on left side, dual vacuum windshield wipers, and cowl ventilator
· Deluxe cab: door ventilating wings, rear quarter windows, sun visor on left side, dual vacuum windshield wipers, and cowl ventilator
· Custom cab: door ventilator wings, rear quarter window, dome light, armrest on left door, dual interior sun visors, airfoam rubber seat padding, deluxe seatback, dual electric windshield wipers (on large trucks only), and cowl ventilator

The B series made its debut with all-new styling, the keynote of which was a combination of massive strength and smooth flowing lines. From the front, an appearance of lowness and ruggedness was emphasized by the broad horizontal stainless steel louvers that extended across the radiator grille and also by the clean horizontal sweep across the tops of the fenders. The radiator grille was a one-piece stamping that extended across the front fender housings. The front fender housings extended back from the radiator grille panel,

Upholstery material was a long-lasting leather-like vinyl. A wide chair-height seat and flat floor provided comfortable seating for three big men. Dodge lined the entire cab interior in soft cardboard-type material for comfort and warmth.

and the lines carried into the cab doors, accentuating their modern streamlining. Wide-set headlights mounted into the grille panel served to illuminate the width of the truck to approaching vehicles.

B series Dodge pickup bodies were now full-size, a feature all other manufacturers would copy. The most important feature of the new pickups was more cargo room. On half-ton models, bodies grew to 49in wide and to 54in wide on the three-quarter and one-ton sizes. Sides grew higher also to 22-1/16in at the top of the flareboards, and to 19-15/16in at the top of the tailgate, allowing plenty of room for even big loads. Truck owners appreciated the combination of strength, longer life, and larger load-carrying ability the larger bodies provided.

New cycle-type rear fenders provided a convenient step into or out of the truck from over the side. Long, wide steel running boards also provided ample space to stand on when loading or unloading from the side of the truck.

The B series included an attractive panel model. Exceptionally rugged, roomy, and streamlined, its 55in

B series-type Practical pickup boxes were retained for C series pickups. A step-type rear bumper was an extra-cost option, although it was seldom purchased. Standard paint design included a black cargo box, rear fenders, and running boards, regardless of cab color. For a slight extra charge, buyers could choose to have the cargo box and rear fenders painted cab color. Restyled rear fenders were new for 1953.

height easily accommodated tall and bulky loads. Buyers could choose from two panel models, standard and deluxe. Deluxe models included door ventilating wings, sun visor on the right side, armrest on the left door, and dual electric windshield wipers.

1950 Dodge B Series

Dodge's B-2 series was announced in October 1949. Two important innovations included fluid drive and a cleaned-up cab floor.

For the first time, a steering column-mounted three-speed transmission shift lever became standard

Left
Dodge built C series Functional Design pickups from 1954 through 1956. A 1954 half-ton C6-1-B-108 is shown. Hallmarks of C series pickups included a rounder, more contemporary design of cab and fenders, one-piece windshield, and overall cab height reduction of 3in. Frames and steering mechanisms were re-engineered, but drivetrains carried over unchanged. Late in the model year, a powerful overhead-valve V-8 engine was introduced as an extra-cost option on all light-duty trucks. At that time, the 230ci L-head six became the standard six; up to then, all half- and three-quarter-ton trucks were powered by the 218ci, 100hp L-head six.

equipment. To complement the new shift lever, the parking brake lever was changed to the redesigned "right spot" lever. It was mounted under the edge of the dashboard and handily located to the driver's right. Pulling the lever straight out set the brake; rotating it one-quarter turn clockwise and releasing it took the brake off.

The combination of the steering column-mounted shift lever and right spot handbrake lever cleared the floor from all obstructions and allowed legroom for a passenger seated in the center of the seat, and it allowed easy entry through the right door.

1951–1952 Dodge B Series

The first significant B series appearance change occurred with the B-3 series introduced on Saturday, February 19, 1951. New front sheet metal gave the three-year-old B series a more pleasing appearance. For the first time, Dodge stylists stamped the Job-Rated slogan into a chrome-plated medallion located in the middle of the grille. New front bumper and optional grille guards helped provide a feeling of added massiveness. The bumper ends wrapped around more of the fender to give greater protection. Larger parking lights located below the headlights also served as turn signal lights.

65

The 1954 restyled instrument panel featured a glovebox located in the center of the panel within easy reach of the driver. At this point in time, Dodge Truck's export sales were brisk. The balanced instrument panel design lent itself to either right- or left-hand drive.

The new front-end style gave an impression of greater width and massiveness. Driver visibility improved due to lowering the hood slightly. The Dodge Ram hood ornament became an extra-cost option. Dodge engineering repositioned the windshield wiper arms to allow the blades more coverage, and when not in use, they rested in a horizontal position at the base of the windshield.

Cab interior improvements included a new instrument panel design that arranged all instruments in a cluster immediately in front of the driver where they could be seen at a glance. Also, for better instrument visibility, light ivory dial numerals were used to create a contrast with the green background on the facings. The instrument panel continued to be finished in the same paint color as the cab.

To provide extra driver comfort, the steering wheel was moved back and down for a more natural driving position. In addition, an attractive chrome steering wheel horn ring was included as standard on light-duty models only.

Major mechanical updates included raising the engine's compression ratio to 7.0:1 and total horsepower to 97; the radiator bypass was built into the water pump and cylinder block; a narrower, low-friction fan belt replaced the former wide type; four-speed transmissions were now of the synchro-shift type for easier and quieter operation.

1953 Dodge B Series

New B-4 series Dodge trucks went on display on Thursday, December 4, 1952. Visitors in Dodge showrooms saw a new line of Dodge trucks loaded with new features—new styling, new cab interior colors, new automatic transmission, and more. Although decorative striping was omitted from the grille, new chrome rims for headlights and parking lights added a sparkle to front-end styling. Chrome headlight trim had been replaced by paint during the Korean War years.

For the first time, Dodge-Tint glass was available for all windows. Dodge-Tint glass had a pleasant green tint that absorbed heat, making the cab cooler in hot weather. The tint also reduced sun glare and glare from oncoming traffic.

Pickups sported a new streamlined rear fender that molded smoothly into the body. In the opinion of most

Dodge buffs, however, the new fenders detracted from the pickup's beauty and distinctiveness. One-ton models, equipped with dual rear wheels, continued to use the old-style fenders.

The biggest news for 1953 was the all-new 116in wheelbase half-ton B-116 model. Its 7-1/2ft cargo box and 56cu-ft of load space provided the greatest load space of any half-ton pickup. Adding the B-116 long-box half-ton pickup gave Dodge Truck another first: Dodge was the first of the Big Three to market short-box and long-box half-ton pickups.

Without a doubt, Dodge's most important innovation for 1953 had to be its Truck-O-Matic transmission with Gyrol Fluid Drive. Dodge called it a self-shifting transmission and made it available on all half-ton and three-quarter-ton trucks.

1954–1955 Dodge C-1 Series

Powerful new V-8 engines and modern styling highlighted 1954's C-1 series. Their new appearance was most evident in the lower cab height which was achieved by setting the cab lower on the frame. Modern curved lines replaced the angular characteristic of the B series. V-8 engines, although not available in light-duty trucks at introduction time, became available as an extra-cost option late in the model year.

The overall appearance of the new C-1 series suggested massiveness and motion. Wide-spaced headlights provided a better outline of the truck's width. Engineering reduced overall height by 3in as a result of chassis improvements and redesigned springs. Shorter height provided reduced loading heights and a lower center of gravity for better stability and handling. A welcomed feature was the new one-piece curved windshield for better vision. Wider front treads and new frames, which curved in at the front wheels to create a recess for the steering gear, increased clearance between the front wheels and frame to provide stability and greater maneuverability. Dodge offered a 39deg turning angle, right or left. A new steering-gear-before-axle-linkage position insulated the steering column and steering wheel from road shocks by rear shackling of the front springs.

Dodge continued using the term Pilot-House to designate 1954 cabs. Dodge design engineers created a safer and more comfortable cab than ever before by adding to door width and height for easier entry and exit. Windowsills lowered to elbow height increased driver comfort, and vent wings became standard equipment.

Bodies

The standard pickup body continued to be the low-side body, while high-side bodies could be ordered on all models at extra cost. Most buyers ordered their new Dodge pickup with a high-side body. An optional rear step-type bumper replaced the former straight type. The spare tire carrier was underslung. Unless the buyer of a B series truck wanted to pay extra, the truck's rear fenders and pickup body came in black regardless of cab color. For the C series this was true only on half-ton mod-

"Truck-O-Matic" is an extremely rare nameplate on Dodge pickups of this era. Only 1953 through early 1955 production half- and three-quarter-ton trucks could be equipped with this unique extra-cost option. A retail price of $110 placed it out of reach of most buyers. Truck-O-Matic was the same semi-automatic transmission Chrysler and DeSoto automobiles of the day were equipped with.

els, while three-quarter and one-ton rear fenders and pickup box matched the cab color at no extra cost. Chrome metallic painted wheels were standard on light-duty trucks.

Engines and Transmissions

At the beginning of the model year, both light-duty L-head six-cylinder engines (218ci and 230ci) were unchanged.

A three-speed synchro-shift was the standard transmission for half-ton models, and a heavy-duty three-speed synchro-shift was standard for three-quarter and one-ton models. A four-speed synchro-shift was an option on all light-duty models. Fluid drive was offered on all light-duty trucks, while Truck-O-Matic was limited to half- and three-quarter-ton models.

In August 1954, at the end of the model year, a 241ci overhead-valve V-8 became an option on all light-duty models except Power Wagon and Route Van. The

Following pages
The W series Power Wagon's styling mirrored that of all other conventional cab trucks. Two exceptions included the fact that Power Wagon's front fenders came from medium-duty trucks to lend an air of bigness, and Power Wagon nameplates were used on both sides of the hood.

Conventional cab Power Wagons differed from the original in nearly every way. One of the biggest differences was its available, extra-cost 315ci, 204hp V-8 engine. Another was its ex-

tra-cost fully automatic transmission, which was offered only with the V-8 engine. The truck shown has a four-speed transmission.

new V-8 was called Power Dome, but it was not a Hemi. It was the same block used on the optional Hemi in one and a half-, two-, and two and a half-ton mediums, but

Finally, in 1957 Dodge began using model number plates to identify nominal size ratings. Three-quarter-ton models, whether two-wheel drive or four-wheel drive, were "200s." The double V insignia was a corporate identity symbol standing for "Forward Look." Forward Look meant a contemporary styling that made Chrysler's vehicles appear to be in motion even while at rest. The double V drew attention to the fact that the company was into modern overhead-valve V-8 engines in a big way.

with a single rocker arm. It was advertised at 145hp and billed as the most powerful engine available in any light-duty truck.

In spite of an all-new design, the use of Hemi-powered engines in medium- and heavy-duty trucks, and the introduction of the most powerful V-8 in the light-duty truck field, 1954 was not a good year for Dodge. Sales at 60,658 were down 26.3 percent from the year before. Total industry sales declined by 12.2 percent. Only Ford enjoyed a sales increase over 1953. Total North American production was 102,088, most of which (91,197) were built in Detroit. A total of 3,690 vehicles were built in San Leandro, and 7,201 in Canada.

Right
Dodge Truck's first four-wheel-drive conventional cab models were 1957 half- and three-quarter-ton Power Wagons (the three-quarter-ton is shown). Conventional cab W series Power Wagons were engineered from the frames up for four-wheel-drive service, but they are totally different from the original military-type Power Wagon. Dodge management sensed a market shift to four-wheel-drive light-duty vehicles. These trucks were designed to capture a larger part of that market. Dodge was already the recognized four-wheel-drive leader. A one-ton conventional cab model was added in 1958.

This two-tone red-and-white paint design was the 1957 Dodge D100 Sweptside pickup's "signature" colors. A standard tailgate had to be slightly modified to fit between these special fenders. Rear bumper and rear fenders are from a two-door Dodge Suburban station wagon.

1955–1956 Dodge C-3 Series

All-new 1954 C-1 series Dodge trucks remained essentially unchanged for one and a half years. The only difference between 1954 and 1955 models was the addition of the V-8 engine, which became available late in 1954. Factory list prices didn't even change; a half-ton six-cylinder low-side pickup in 1955 still cost the same $1,331 as it did a year earlier.

In April 1955, Dodge announced an all-new C-3 truck series. The C-3 series featured new cabs, colors, models, engines, transmissions, and power options. Dodge took a major step forward in glamorizing, modernizing, and making light-duty trucks more car-like in appearance and performance.

Left
This American classic pickup may well be the most highly recognizable Dodge collector truck of all time. It was a late-in-the-model year introduction, a fact which held total production down to only 2,000 units. One would never dream that attaching an automobile's rear fenders to the sides of a pickup's box would turn out so well. In retrospect, the rear fenders appear to have been designed for the truck instead of for a station wagon.

Even though considerably changed from the C-1 series, the C-3 series was evolutionary, not revolutionary. New cabs, for example, while basically the same, now featured a wraparound windshield and rear window. The windshield boasted 1,023sq-in of glass and a total of 2,321sq-in of glass in the windshield, rear window, and side windows. Dodge called this Full-Circle Visibility.

The top edge of the cab roof projected slightly forward to form a stylish eyebrow, and a chrome-plated molding on custom regal cabs gave this top-of-the-line model greater beauty and distinction.

A simple, tasteful chrome-plated V-8 medallion placed on the center of the hood just above the grille opening identified V-8-powered trucks. The speedometer recorded up to 110mph, an accommodation to the added power and speed of the nimble new V-8 engine.

Engines and Transmissions

The 230ci L-6 remained unchanged and served as the standard engine for all light-duty trucks. Later in the model year, the L-6's compression ratio increased to 7.6:1, bringing horsepower up to 115. A 0.1255in larger bore boosted the V-8's displacement to 259ci and horsepower to 169. The industry's biggest and

Standard engine for 1957 Dodge half-ton pickups was the
230ci, 120hp L-head six-cylinder.

Sweptsides look as good going as coming. All four taillights are fully functional.

most powerful V-8 just became even more dominant in the low-tonnage category.

For the first time, half-ton models became available with optional three-speed manual transmission with overdrive. Also, for the first time on light-duty models (including forward control models), a fully automatic transmission was available. PowerFlite automatic eliminated the clutch pedal. PowerFlite consisted of an efficient torque converter, with a simple, fully automatic two-speed planetary gear transmission. The transmission gear selector lever was conveniently mounted on the steering column. Fluid drive was dropped.

Bodies

Early in the model year, buyers could choose either a high-side or a low-side half-ton pickup body, while only high-side bodies were available on three-quarter- and one-ton pickups. Late in the model year, however, engineering changed from flare sideboards to a flat top, and subsequently the low-side pickup body was discontinued.

Power Wagon continued without changes for 1955–56. Dodge truck sales and production for 1955 moved ahead of 1954's totals. Sales increased by 9.1 percent to 66,208, and production inched up to 95,618, less than a 1 percent increase. All U.S. truck production was consolidated in Michigan; the California plant ceased building trucks.

In July, production stopped when the summer's extreme heat caused production workers to walk off the job, and production stopped again in the fall due to an axle shortage caused by a strike at the Eaton Manufacturing Company.

Sales and production figures for 1956 fell below 1955's numbers. Sales fell 12.9 percent to 57,651, and production decreased 4.4 percent to 91,383.

1957 Dodge K Series

Sixty-five percent of the 10.5 million trucks in use in 1957 were light-duty trucks, 9,000lb GVW and under. Therefore, Dodge paid special attention to that huge market segment in designing 1957 models.

Dodge light-duty truck engines for 1957 featured big boosts in horsepower. The 230ci L-6 increased from 115 to 120hp. The optional V-8 was a new 315ci engine, producing 204hp.

Another industry first for Dodge light-duty trucks was LoadFlite push-button controlled three-speed automatic transmission. LoadFlite gave passenger-car driving ease to Dodge light-duty trucks.

An alligator-type hood replaced the former butterfly hood. Exclusive to Dodge, the hood would open to a full 90deg position and made it possible to service any part of the engine, even remove it, without removing the hood. The hood could also be opened to a 48deg position for normal servicing.

A 12-volt electrical system was standard on all models for better engine performance and easier starting.

The hood ornament for 1957 was a wide V at the front for V-8 models. For the first time in Dodge history, a plate with the model number incorporated graced the sides of both front fenders. Model designations began with D100 for half-ton, D200 for three-quarter-ton, and D300 for one-ton. Dodge referred to model size by numerical designations rather than by nominal rating. Later, when half-, three-quarter-, and one-ton four-wheel-drive models with standard cab styling were added, D100 designated two-wheel-drive models and W100 designated four-wheel-drive models.

Extra-cost power steering and power brakes contributed to passenger car driving ease.

Throughout the fifties, the Dodge pickup cab's interior paint design was always the cab's exterior color. Red-and-white upholstery colors coordinated perfectly with exterior colors.

Conventional Cab Power Wagons

Over the eleven years that Dodge built Power Wagons, the company had received so many requests for bigger and smaller versions of this versatile truck it finally expanded the four-wheel-drive line. In 1956, the two-ton brother to the Power Wagon was introduced, and late in the 1957 model year (May) two smaller models followed: the W100 half-ton truck built on either a 108in or 116in wheelbase and the bigger W200 three-quarter-ton truck built on a 116in wheelbase.

Both new models featured optional V-8 power and automatic transmissions and enabled Dodge to tighten its hold on the four-wheel-drive market.

The original Power Wagon continued unchanged except that power steering and power brakes became an available option and ignition key starting was standard. The 230ci L-6 was given a boost to 113hp by increasing its compression ratio to 7.9:1. The original Power Wagon would never be upgraded to V-8 power and automatic transmission, but would continue through 1968 in its original form.

In spite of an excellent product offering—new models, new power, and various engineering enhancements—1957 was not a good year for Dodge trucks. The North American production total of 83,977 was down 19 percent from 1956. Dodge Canada built 7,378 of the total. Industry sales overall declined only 4.1 percent from 1956. V-8 engines powered 54 percent of Dodge trucks built in 1957, a strong showing when you consider this was only the fourth year of V-8 engine production in Dodge trucks.

Sweptside D100

Dodge Truck's sales continued their downward trend in 1957. Truck sales had steadily declined from their peak year of 1947. In fact, there were years during the Depression when Dodge enjoyed better sales than during the last five years of the 1950s.

In comparison, Chevrolet's light-duty truck sales for 1955–1957 led the industry. Chevrolet had completely restyled its truck line in 1955 and introduced the innovative Cameo Carrier. Chevrolet's first V-8-powered trucks also featured wraparound windshields and car-like cab amenities.

In 1957, Ford also achieved new sales success. Ford actually enjoyed a sales gain from 1956, making Ford and Mack the only two truck manufacturers to do so in the slight recession year of 1957. Ford also created a lot of light truck excitement with its popular new Ranchero. Ford's entire line was restyled for 1957 and featured a new cab-wide Styleside pickup box, a very attractive truck, the first of its kind.

Dodge, on the other hand, didn't have the capital available to develop a new model to compete with Ford and Chevy. Joe Berr, manager of special equipment sales at the time, knew that Dodge must do something and do it quickly to breathe a little life into a not very exciting truck line. His challenge was to develop something new without spending a lot of money on new tooling and parts, and to move quickly.

Berr had an idea. He went over to the Dodge car assembly plant, appropriated a set of rear fenders and a rear bumper from a 1957 Dodge two-door Suburban station wagon and brought them back to the special equipment shop. In the shop, Berr parked a 1957 long wheelbase custom cab half-ton pickup. Burt Nagos welded the station wagon fenders to the pickup box sides after removing the stock fenders. The station wagon's rear bumper fit like a glove, but the tailgate had to be cut down to fit between the new long fenders. Chrome molding pieces custom-made to fit the cab continued the lines running forward from the station wagon fenders. Add a two-tone paint design, full chrome wheel covers, and wide white sidewalls, and there you have it, one of the most exciting and interesting collector trucks of all time.

A few key Dodge truck dealers evaluated the new creation. "Build it," they all said. "We can sell this beauty!"

1958 Dodge L Series

New L series Dodge trucks were introduced on October 31, 1957. For the second consecutive year, they received an all-new front-end appearance with dramatic new styling. Light-duty models had a handsome new grille, dual headlights, a full-width hood, new bigger bumpers, and rich new chrome trim.

Hoods on the new trucks were made full width for maximum engine cooling and ease of engine servicing. New fender housings and new two-piece engine compartment splash shields yielded the greatest possible engine compartment width. The battery was moved from beneath the driver's floor to under the hood.

Due to the fact that a one-ton four-wheel-drive model with conventional cab styling was added for 1958, the Power Wagon's model number changed to W300M, with M indicating military-type sheet metal.

New models included the one-ton conventional cab W300 Power Wagon and a Power Wagon Town Panel as a companion to the Power Wagon Town Wagon introduced in 1957.

Dodge's style leader continued to be the Sweptside D100 pickup; the flashiest truck on the road became even more attractive with 1958's new styling and colors.

U.S. truck manufacturers suffered with the general business recession in 1958. Total annual output of 871,330 units was the lowest since 1945. This was the first post-World War II year in which the industry failed to produce a million vehicles. The 871,330 total for 1958 represented a 20.1 percent dip from the previous year.

Dodge's production and sales suffered along with the rest of the truck industry. Total output of 58,663 trucks in U.S. plants represented the lowest total since 1938. Dodge Canada built 6,263 trucks.

1959 Dodge M Series

The most important new product for 1959 was the sleek, smooth-sided Sweptline pickup. Sweptline pickups featured a cab-wide cargo box with integral rear fenders. With their full, smooth sweep of body from front to rear, Sweptline pickups captured most-handsome pickup honors for 1959. The original fender side pickup was renamed Utiline and continued as before with its hardwood floor and narrow box.

For the fourth time in just over four years, Dodge introduced yet another new V-8 engine for 1959. The new V-8 was the famous, dependable 318. Dodge called it the Power Dome, Power Giant 318. It was of single rocker arm design with a dome-shaped combustion chamber, but it was not a true Hemi. Double rocker shaft Hemi V-8s powered medium- and heavy-duty Dodge trucks, but 1959 would be the last year for a Hemi engine in Dodge trucks. In 1960, Dodge introduced an entirely new family of V-8 engines for large trucks. The 230ci L-6 soldiered on without change.

U.S. truck manufacturers rebounded from 1958's recession by building 30 percent more trucks in 1959 and topping one million units again. Industry total was 1,137,401. Dodge rebounded by increasing production by 22.2 percent, topping off at 71,580 for U.S. factories. Dodge Canada built 6,087 additional units. Sales surged 40.7 percent.

1960 Dodge P Series

Dodge introduced all-new medium- and high-tonnage trucks for 1960. The United States had completed much of its new interstate freeway system, which proved to be an important advantage for the trucking industry. Allowable truck GVWs and GCWs increased, as did average speeds, allowing over-the-road trucks to become larger and more powerful. Dodge positioned itself in the marketplace to capitalize on this new market with new products.

Dodge marked time in 1960 with light-duty models as the company busily prepared for an all-new light-duty model for 1961. Light-duty models for 1960 received a facelift with a bright metal grille, a new sound-proofed cab headliner, and a new extra-heavy-duty three-speed manual transmission.

U.S. truck industry production in 1960 increased only 5 percent over 1959, while Dodge production (at 70,305) fell 1.9 percent from 1959. A close examination of production figures by weight class, however, shows that Dodge actually produced more half-ton trucks in 1960 than in 1959 (33,179 in 1960 versus 30,758 in 1959).

When photographed in July 1995, this twenty-one-year-old Dodge NCT900 LCF transfer-dump was still in everyday service in Los Angeles. This "high cab" truck is powered by a Detroit Diesel engine. It stands out because of its aluminum or chrome-plated fuel tanks, front bumper, grille, sun visor, and short rear fenders. *Stan Holtzman*

Chapter 6

Big Dodge Trucks
1960–1975

The original Dodge Brothers Company began building big trucks (medium-duty two-ton six-cylinder powered) through its wholly owned subsidiary, Graham Brothers, as early as 1927. At that time, however, all trucks built by the company were badged as Graham Brothers. In 1927, Dodge management had turned all truck building responsibility over to the truck division because the overtaxed factories couldn't keep up with the demand for automobiles. Truck building was moved out of Dodge Main's factories and off-site.

Unlike its two major Big Three rivals, Dodge always had access to every engine the corporation built, before Dodge Brothers was sold to Chrysler Corporation and after. Ford and Chevrolet limited engine availability to those used in their respective car lines until the late 1940s for Ford and well into the 1950s for Chevrolet. Consequently, Ford and Chevrolet's truck offerings did not surpass two-ton models.

Graham Brothers truck building division of Dodge Brothers began using a six-cylinder Dodge car engine for two-ton trucks in 1927. Six-cylinder-powered three-ton trucks and buses were added in 1928. Equipped with a four-speed transmission and four-wheel hydraulic brakes, these trucks were marvelous, fast, powerful, and easy to stop.

Graham Brothers trucks were renamed Dodge Brothers trucks early in 1929, six months after being purchased by Chrysler. One year later, Dodge Truck inherited the former Chrysler Imperial 310ci, 96hp big block six-cylinder engine for three-ton trucks.

A second Chrysler Imperial engine (still current at the time in Imperial cars) was handed down to Dodge Truck in 1932: the huge 385ci, 115hp straight eight L-head engine. Dodge used this engine for a new four-ton truck series. Dodge Truck, however, dropped the eight after the 1934 model year and reverted to the 310ci, 96hp big block L-head six for three-ton trucks, its largest truck series.

A three-ton truck was the largest model built until 1950, except for four-ton custom-built Airflow trucks, which actually used the same drivetrain as three-ton trucks.

Dodge's sensational engine introduction rocked the truck industry in 1939. Dodge was not a major factor in the heavy-duty truck business, yet the company introduced a three-ton diesel truck with an engine designed, engineered, and built by Chrysler Corporation. In 1939, diesel-powered trucks were still somewhat of a rarity. Diesels had a small share of the market, but they were beginning to make an impact. One wonders if the impact was significant enough to warrant the expense of engineering and building a diesel engine in-house. At the time, Chrysler Corporation was dominated by engineers whose goal was to be always on the cutting edge of technology.

The Dodge diesel was a four-stroke, 331ci, 95hp, overhead-valve six-cylinder producing 226lb-ft of maximum torque at 1000rpm. Its general dimensions, mountings, and crankcase structure were identical with those of the six-cylinder 331ci gasoline engine, permitting economies in the manufacturing and installation of the engine. Internally, the two engines were completely different; no parts interchanged between the two.

Dodge built the diesel from 1939 to 1942 for trucks and continued to build it for industrial purposes during World War II. The diesel did not return after the war.

Dodge Truck made a big splash in the medium- and heavy-duty segments in 1954 with the introduction of powerful Hemi V-8 engines. Between 1954 and 1959, Dodge Truck offered five Hemi V-8 engines: 241ci, 270ci, 315ci, 331ci, and 354ci. The three smaller engines powered medium-duty trucks, and the two larger engines powered heavy-duty trucks. A Hemi was never available in light-duty trucks. With the Hemi engines, Dodge had a situation similar to that of thirty-five years later when it introduced Cummins turbo-diesel-powered pickups. Dodge had the industry's hottest engine, and it didn't take long for truckers to catch on.

Dodge's Power Giant 354, a 354ci Hemi V-8 producing 234 maximum gross horsepower and 360lb-ft maximum gross torque when equipped with twin carburetors and dual exhausts, was rated for a maximum GVW of 30,000lb and a maximum GCW rating of 65,000lb in tractor-trailer service. Or, when powering a T900 tandem-axle truck, maximum GVW was 49,000lb and 65,000lb maximum GCW in tractor-trailer service. Independent operators purchased the big Dodges for far less money than the expensive brands and then ran rings around them. Dodge tractor's free-breathing Hemi V-8 engines ran the road in less time, at lower cost, and chalked up more round trips per day putting more dollars in the owner's pocket.

Dodge Truck jumped into the heavy-duty truck business with both feet in 1960 with an entirely new series of high-tonnage gasoline and diesel trucks, featuring revolutionary swing-out fenders for the fastest and most convenient engine accessibility in the industry. Dodge built both medium- and heavy-duty trucks in the new low-cab-forward design. Dodge engineers chose the swing-out fender design over a tilt cab for cost reasons; their solution cost less and therefore was more cost effective.

The new C model trucks increased Dodge's GVW ratings up to 53,000lb and increased GCW ratings up to 76,800lb with either gasoline or diesel engines. Dodge management was determined to play an increasingly important role in the heavy-duty market in the future. Forces driving the heavy-duty truck market included the fact that much of the interstate freeway system was in place, which created an opportunity for trucks to wrest a considerable amount of interstate freight business away from the railroads. The other factor favoring big trucks was the ascendancy of the diesel engine. Diesels were more fuel efficient, and because

To many observers of Dodge trucks, Airflow models are the epitome of big truck style and grace. Airflows came to be because of a suggestion made to management by an admirer of Chrysler's Airflow cars. He thought the Airflow car's modern design would make an exceptionally well-styled truck. Management agreed and put the program in place. Airflows were custom-built trucks; their bodies were essentially built by hand. Engines, transmissions, axles, and so on were shared with heavy-duty trucks. Most Airflows went into tanker service, but some were employed in other industries. A 1938 four-ton is shown.

Dodge built this top-of-the-line three-ton WRA series only in 1946 and 1947. It is rated for a maximum GVW of 23,000lb and maximum GCW of 40,000lb when used in tractor-trailer service. Dodge created this series from lessons learned building 15,000 heavy-duty trucks for the Chinese during World War II. That truck, the T234, started in production in October 1944 and continued until March 1946. The WRA is an example of a truck originally engineered and built for the military converted to a successful civilian truck after completing the military contract. A 1947 Dodge WRA three-ton tractor with 331ci L-head six-cylinder engine, five-speed transmission, and two-speed rear axle is shown.

they were built heavier, they simply lasted longer. Nevertheless, the gasoline engine still reigned supreme in 1960. Even in the heaviest weight classes, more gasoline-powered trucks were sold than diesels, but the ratio was changing rapidly.

Dodge engineers chose four diesel engines from Cummins, the industry leader, to power their new heavyweights. Dodge also introduced five new gasoline engines for medium- and heavy-duty trucks. Hemi V-8s were dropped at the end of the 1959 model year.

1964 Heavy-Duty L Tilt Cabs

In February 1964, Dodge started production of an all new, heavy-duty tilt cab truck engineered to fill a niche for a high-quality truck able to move maximum loads at top legal speeds for long distances. It was a truck for truckers who knew and demanded maximum safety, performance, load capacity, durability, ease of maintenance, and low operating costs. It boasted one of the shortest cabs in the industry in 1964. The new heavy-duty L tilt cab was constructed of riveted aluminum panels with a fiberglass skirt to assure maximum lightness, durability, and resistance to corrosion. Available only with diesel power, a first for Dodge, the L series tilts were built to accept a wide variety of diesel engines—sixes as well as V-8s—from Cummins, Detroit Diesel, and Caterpillar.

Six L models comprised the line; three single-axle units and three tandem-axle models. Three cab styles were also included: the 49in standard cab and sleepers with either a 24in- or a 30in-wide sleeping compartment. Wheelbases from 98in to 200in were offered to meet the many requirements of the trucking industry.

Cabs were built of aluminum for light weight to allow maximum payloads and a long life free from rust. In addition to quality construction, comfort and safety were built into the cab and particular attention was given to insulating the cab to provide optimum heat and sound isolation for driver comfort.

Maximum ease of maintenance was designed into the L tilts. Its cab could be tilted 55deg for maximum accessibility to the engine compartment. Maintenance checks of water and oil could be performed without tilting the cab. The cab tilt mechanism was hydraulic. At maximum tilt, the entire engine and radiator could be removed easily.

1966 Medium-Duty Tilt Cab

Dodge introduced one of the lowest priced medium-duty tilt cabs in its field. It was available as a straight truck or as a tractor in two models: L600 with GVWs ranging from 17,000lb to 24,000lb, and L700 with GVWs of 18,500lb and 27,500lb. Engine options in the L600 ranged from the 140hp, 225 premium slant six to the 186hp, 361ci premium V-8 and included the 131hp Perkins 6-354 diesel. L700's engine choices included the 194hp 361-3 V-8 and 217hp 413-2 V-8.

Dodge engineers adopted the attractive A100 pickup's cab for this tilt cab series. Its short, actually nonexistent, hood moved the driver all the way forward for

Dodge heavy-duty Hemi engine-powered trucks continued through model year 1959. Model D900 (shown) was rated for a maximum GCW of 65,000lb in tractor-trailer service. It was powered by a Power Giant 354 Hemi V-8 engine, which pro-duced 234hp and 360lb-ft of maximum torque at 2400rpm. Dual carbs and exhausts were standard, as was an extra-heavy-duty five-speed transmission. A three- or four-speed optional auxiliary transmission provided up to twenty forward speeds.

Dodge Truck headed in a whole new direction in the 1960 model year by entering the heavy-duty diesel truck market. Playing a big part in this new line were the LCF (Low Cab Forward) medium- and heavy-duty gas or diesel models. Here is a 1960 C700 tandem-axle medium-duty gas tractor-trailer.

maximum visibility, with the engine behind him so that the cab would accommodate three passengers. To guard against cab heat, across the entire underbody was a thick barrier of insulation, plus there were pads under the floor mat, in the roof, and across the dash panel. The medium-duty L's cab was one of the coolest and quietest on the market.

Its short 74.5in BBC (bumper to back of cab) dimension and 50deg wheel turn angle provided great maneuverability. Its short cab, short wheelbases, and 50deg turn angle were all factors that made this Dodge tilt a real swivel-hip hauler for snaking through city streets and alleys. With an 89in wheelbase, it could actually make U-turns in streets only 28ft wide.

A simple bar released and unlocked the cab, allowing a 45deg tilt for easy access to the engine. Large counterbalancing coil springs aided in boosting the lightweight cab forward for clear access to the rearward-placed engine, clutch, and transmission.

1975 Dodge Bighorn CNT950

Major goals for the design of the Bighorn set by Dodge engineers were to make it a premium-quality truck for both fleet service and individual owner-operators, to be long-lived, rugged, and easy to maintain.

The long-nose conventional 950 was a heavy-duty diesel engine model only. Designed with the latest technical innovations, the 950 was capable of accommodating all then current diesel engines up to 475hp. A large selection of axles, transmissions, frames, brakes, and other components from the industry's leading manufacturers could be specified. Every heavy-duty truck in Dodge's line was custom built to the owner's specifications. The owner selected every mechanical component, cab interior detail, exterior and interior paint, and finish design.

The instrument panel was hinged on the bottom and swung downward for access to electrical connections, tubing, valves, and instruments. The tilting steering column had to be lowered to open the panel fully.

To keep the cost of replacement parts low, Dodge designed the 950 with as few special factory-built parts as possible. In almost every case where new metal parts were required, construction was of the bend-and-weld type, permitting easy repair.

Engine access was simplified with the forward-tilting, fiberglass front end. The hood's ram's head ornament served as a handle to pull forward the counterbalanced hood. There was enough space between the tire and frame to give a mechanic access to the engine.

1975 Dodge Bighorn 900 Conventional

The long conventional Bighorn 950 introduced in 1973 continued in production, but was joined by the 1975 Bighorn 900 conventional, also termed the "Super C."

It was built on wheelbases ranging from 134in up to 212in; GVW ranged from 28,000 to 60,000lb; power rating ranged from 230hp to 350hp diesel engines only—Detroit Diesel and Cummins engines.

The Bighorn 900 met all government regulations for airbrakes and noise control and had Rockwell-Standard's Skid-Trol computerized brake control system to meet federal brake regulations.

To comply with new interior noise regulations, Dodge Bighorn 900 included improved insulation and seating.

Like the Bighorn 950, the Bighorn 900 featured a rugged heavy-gauge reinforced steel cab and a forward tilting, reinforced fiberglass hood.

Super C models would have replaced the top-of-the-line C cab-forward heavy-duty trucks. But it was not to be because Dodge Truck management elected to retreat

The biggest 1960 LCF model was this NCT1000 five-ton diesel-powered tandem-axle chassis cab. Heavy-duty trucks were custom built to the buyer's specifications. Dodge offered axles, transmissions, brakes, diesel engines, wheels, and other components from the finest component manufacturers to allow buyers to specify trucks to fit their hauling requirements. NCT1000 diesel-powered tandem-axle models equipped with fifth-wheel equipment carried a maximum GCW rating of 76,800lb, the highest legal gross weight allowed on the nation's freeways.

from the heavy-duty truck business. Heavy-duty trucks had been only marginally profitable at Dodge for years. Since the inception of the wildly successful and profitable Club Cab pickup in 1973, which the company couldn't make enough of, management opted to concentrate on the profitable light-duty and medium-duty trucks (Dodge vans and wagons were also selling extremely well at the time). Only a handful of Bighorn 900s were built before heavy-duty truck production ceased.

Management dropped all cab-forward C trucks, both medium- and heavy-duty models, but retained the conventional cab medium-duty model which was new in 1974. Since Dodge's heavy-duty truck era began in 1960, Dodge continued to build two medium-duty truck series: cab-forward C models and conventional cab (same cab as pickups) models. Conventional cab (D model) medium-duty models remained in production only through the 1977 model year. Chrysler Corporation, however, continues to build medium-duty Dodge and Fargo trucks to this day at its Mexican plant. These are for sale in Mexico and for export to Latin American countries.

The biggest Dodge trucks were the 1973 to 1975 long conventional Bighorn diesel-only-powered trucks. Dodge Bighorn featured clean, simple, and functional styling. They were the most advanced, most highly engineered heavy-duty Dodge trucks ever built. Every Bighorn was custom built to the buyer's special trucking needs.

Chapter 7

Sweptline Trucks
1961–1971

"Hauls like a truck, handles like the family car," boasted Dodge's advertising slogan for its all-new light-duty truck line for 1961. New styling, chassis, steering, suspension system, and six-cylinder engine combined to create the exciting 1961 Dodge trucks. The half-ton pickup line even received a new name, Dart, which was borrowed from Dodge's highly successful standard-size car series introduced in 1960 and continued into 1961. Oddly enough, Dodge used the Dart name on its pickup line for only one year.

The 1961 Dodge half-ton model's wheelbases were stretched to 114in and 122in versus the former 108in and 116in. Three-quarter-ton models went from 116in to 122in, and one-ton models from 116in to 133in. Longer wheelbase lengths added to riding comfort.

Lowering cab floors by 3in aided entry and exit from the all-new Drivemaster cabs. By redesigning the frame and cab, a 7in reduction was made to overall cab height, plus cab width was stretched 4in allowing the seat to be a full 60in wide, enough for three big men.

The new cab greenhouse featured a larger wraparound windshield and a full-width rear window that tilted inward to minimize the glare of following headlights. Excellent driver visibility resulted from this spacious greenhouse.

Front-end styling was broad and massive because the wide flat hood extended from fender edge to fender edge, giving an uninterrupted line across the width of

Dodge Truck's 1961 D100 half-ton Dart pickup was an all-new truck. Even a new name, in this case borrowed from a Dodge car model, was a first for a two-wheel-drive half-ton pickup. The pickup shown is a top-of-the-line model: white cab roof, full wheel covers, wide white sidewalls, chrome bumper and grille, and large back window. *Chrysler Corporation*

the truck. Dual headlights combined with a newly styled egg-crate grille contributed to the truck's exceptionally fine front appearance.

A well laid-out instrument panel placed all gauges directly in front of the driver. The gauges were calibrated so they pointed vertically under normal conditions for fast, at-a-glance checking. The LoadFlite automatic transmission control continued to be push-button, placed on the far left of the instrument cluster. The instrument cluster used on medium-tonnage trucks became an option. It included an electric tachometer and graduated oil pressure gauge.

The Sweptline's body grew wider and higher in 1961. Lengths remained the same at 6-1/2ft or 8ft, but overall width increased by 4in, giving a 10 percent greater load area.

Chrysler Corporation's famous and respected slant six engine saw its first use in 1960 Dodge and Plymouth cars. For 1961, it became the standard six-cylinder engine in light-duty trucks. The slant six was tilted 30deg to the right in order to mount the water pump alongside the block to decrease the engine's overall length. This engine was originally designed for Chrysler's new line of compact cars. Designers wanted to maximize passenger space within the car's body; every inch was important.

Slant Six Engine
The slant six featured overhead valves, modified wedge-type combustion chambers, and a highly efficient intake manifold. Its design also allowed easy servicing with all major service items such as air cleaner, dipstick, oil filler cover, and oil filter located within easy reach. The cylinder head cover could be readily removed for tappet adjustment. This was a major improvement over the former L-head six with its tappets hidden on the engine's side behind the hot exhaust manifold.

Dodge engineers designed two versions of the slant six: the 225ci and the 170ci. The 225 became the standard engine for D100, D200, D300, W100, W200, and forward control models. The 170 became an option for D100 and the smallest forward control models only. It was not available for any other trucks. It was intended only for those users who carried light loads and who frequently ran their engines at idle such as in package delivery service. The 170ci was a no-charge option, and Dodge recommended that with this engine the GVW not exceed 4,300lb.

The 251ci L-head six continued to be used as the standard engine in W300M Power Wagon and one-ton W300 four-wheel drives with conventional cabs. In addition, the L-6 powered several medium-duty models including school buses and the larger four-wheel-drive two-ton model W500.

At last the sturdy reliable L-head small-block six was retired. This engine had served since 1933, a run of twenty-seven years. When introduced in 1933, it had a displacement of 189.8ci and grew to 230.2ci by 1960.

Model year 1961 proved to be a bad year for truck manufacturers as total production by U.S. makers reached only 1,127,505 units, a drop of 5.9 percent from 1960's total of 1,198,112. Dodge's total production of 64,886 fell 7.7 percent from 1960. Dodge, however, was hurt by a short-lived strike in December 1960, which caused a loss of production.

Of Dodge's 1961 truck production, 71.9 percent of buyers chose six-cylinder engines and 28.1 percent chose V-8 engines. Industry figures showed 6.5 percent for four-cylinder engines, 69.7 percent for six-cylinder, and 23.8 percent for V-8 engines. Dodge also tested a multifuel-burning turbine engine during this year for medium-tonnage application.

Due to soft business conditions, Dodge did not raise truck prices for 1961. Some prices actually fell. The half-ton Dart pickup's price stayed the same as that of the 1960 model half-ton pickup. Dodge truck prices ranged from a low of $1,812 for a D100 Utiline 6-1/2ft pickup to $16,654 for its largest model, the giant tandem 200in wheelbase, NCT-1000 cab-forward diesel.

1962 Dodge S Series
Dodge light-duty trucks generate huge profits for Chrysler Corporation because of their large volume, ex-

cellent unit profit margins, and no retooling costs for annual new model introductions. Truck buyers do not want or expect annual changes merely to keep up with the latest fashion. Now entering the second year of a new model, Dodge held changes to the bare minimum. The challenge was to massage the basic package to entice potential light-truck buyers into Dodge showrooms.

Appearance changes included the addition of a new one-piece steel grille painted Sand Dune White on standard cabs and chrome-plated on custom cabs, moving the Dodge nameplate to the side of each front fender, and adding a model number plate in the center of the grille.

The industry bounced back in 1962, gaining 9.4 percent in total production topping off at 1,240,168 units. Dodge outperformed the industry, gaining 48.1 percent in production for a total of 96,102 units. Dodge's market share jumped from 5.75 percent to 7.66 percent.

During the 1961 model year, Dodge management adopted a policy saying it would make running changes or engineering changes only in the medium- and heavy-duty truck lines. In 1962, after a three-year study, Dodge announced that it would abandon the annual introduction of new models in favor of bringing out engineering improvements whenever they were ready. Management felt that dropping the annual changeover would also eliminate some changes in styling made merely for the sake of having a new model.

1963 Dodge T Series
In keeping with Dodge's new policy of no annual model changes, the 1963 models remained, for all practical purposes, unchanged. No appearance changes, inside or out, no new paint colors or engineering improvements highlighted the new models. In addition, retail prices remained stable, and price reductions made in 1962 continued into 1963. The D100 pickup's price was increased by $9.00, and to the basic truck, equipment worth $13.30 (an oil filter costing $8.60 and a closed crankcase ventilation system priced at $4.70) had been added.

Running improvements during the model year included increased brake lining areas on models D200, P200, W100, W200, D300, and P300. The oil cooler for the LoadFlite automatic transmission was improved to provide more efficient cooling. Power steering became available on V-8 D200 crew cabs as an extra-cost option.

The year turned out to be a good one for Dodge Truck both in terms of production and sales. At 110,987, production for the calendar year represented an increase of 35 percent over 1962. Both export and military sales for the year increased substantially. Dodge's truck plant in Warren, Michigan, recorded the industry's second most productive standing of the year.

For 1963, Dodge built 2,137 diesel-powered trucks, 70,996 six-cylinder trucks, and 37,854 V-8 trucks.

1964 Dodge V Series
In keeping with the policy of no change for change's sake, little was new when Dodge's 1964 models came out in October 1963. At new model introduc-

Dodge's 1964 Custom Sports Special D100 half-ton Sweptline pickup was the industry's first personal Sports Pickup. Dodge's intent was that the CSS would be a multipurpose truck: (1) a rugged hardworking truck for pulling campers, (2) personal transportation for two featuring a plush and comfortable interior with two bucket seats and console, (3) tasteful styling to make it at home in any neighborhood or any situation, and (4) power and performance to suit any lead-foot driver. Engine choices included the adequate 225 slant six, lively 318ci V-8, or the hot 365hp, 426ci high-performance V-8. Twin dual racing stripes extending over the roof and hood indicated this was no ordinary pickup. *Chrysler Corporation*

The Custom Sports Special's all black bucket seats with center console were borrowed from a Dodge car. Black carpet starts on the fire wall, covers the floor, and extends over the gas tank behind the seat.

Instrumentation from a heavy-duty truck, including tachometer, was a requirement with the 426ci V-8. A white steering wheel with chrome horn ring was typical of high-line 1965 pickups.

tion time, mention was made of a new Sport model truck, but the new model did not appear in showrooms until after the first of the year.

Custom Sports Special

The first official announcement from Dodge concerning its new Custom Sports Special pickup came on February 9, 1964. Deliveries to dealers followed in April. Interestingly, this earliest announcement and other early newspaper and magazine articles stated that the largest engine option would be the 413ci V-8. In reality, the high-performance engine turned out to be the 426ci V-8, not the 426 Hemi of racing fame, but nevertheless a potent engine. Rated brake horsepower was 365 at

Left
This second series 1965 Dodge D100 Custom Sports Special is one of only two known trucks equipped with the extra-cost High Performance Engine Package. The 426 V-8 high-performance engine was only offered in 1964 and 1965. This all-black Custom Sports Special pickup with white racing stripes and bright chrome is a striking truck.

4800rpm and maximum torque was 470lb-ft at 3200rpm. A compression ratio of 10.3:1 required the use of premium leaded fuel.

As with any Dodge pickup, the Custom Sports Special's base engine was the 225 slant six, the 318 as the optional V-8, and if buyers wanted to pop for the high-performance package, it included the 426ci V-8, a choice of 3.44 or 3.91 rear axle ratios, heavier (1,250lb versus 1,100lb) rear springs, rear axle struts, a 727 Load-Flite automatic, dual exhausts, heavy-duty instrument cluster, power steering, and a mechanical tachometer.

Custom Sports Specials could be ordered in any Dodge truck standard paint color. The four 1in racing stripes were white on dark-colored models and black on lighter ones. The CSS rode on the 122in wheelbase chassis and was fitted with the 8ft Sweptline cargo box. The 7-1/2ft Utiline box was an option; a three-quarter-ton chassis version was also listed.

Dodge was aware of the tremendous power available with the high-performance engine package, and warranty claims caused real concern. A special bulletin sent to dealers on May 1, 1964, advised them to caution

owners against rapid acceleration of a loaded truck to prevent damage to drivetrain components. Chrysler Corporation assumed no responsibility for repair due to extreme use and operation of the truck. Because the CSS was an optional equipment package and not a specific model, production records are not available to tell how many of these super-powered trucks hit the street.

A100 Compact Trucks

As interesting as the CSS was, the really big news from Dodge for 1964 was the compact truck line. Compact trucks did not become available until late May or early June 1964. Even though Dodge was the last of the Big Three to enter the compact truck business, the company had done its homework well, soon establishing itself as the van leader—a position it has not relinquished to date.

Breaking down the A100 designations, the A became the prefix for a new model, and as usual 100 meant a nominal half-ton rating.

The compact wagon was a little bit different case. Because compact wagons were registered as passenger cars, not trucks, Dodge felt it should use a specific name for these vehicles. The names chosen were Sportsman wagon for the standard wagon and Custom Sportsman wagon for the deluxe wagon.

1965 Dodge A Series

The 1965 Dodge truck story is in reality two completely different stories. The first occurred at the usual new model introduction time in October 1964, when Dodge announced that the entire line carried over unchanged except for the addition of four new engines. Three of these were huge diesels used in heavy-duty models and are not part of our story. The fourth new engine, however, ushered in a whole new era in the compact truck field. It was the first V-8 ever used in a compact van or pickup. This optional 273ci V-8 developed 174hp. At long last, a compact truck offering performance buyers wanted. Now those owners who hauled heavy loads or who used their compact trucks on freeways had the extra power necessary to climb mountain grades and for smooth effortless driving. Dodge engineers squeezed the V-8 into the same "doghouse" that housed the 170ci and 225ci slant sixes, so no space was lost to the new V-8 despite its extra power.

The second 1965 story happened in April when Dodge announced a number of dramatic improvements in the conventional light-duty line. This an-

This A100 pickup is equipped with a Custom Package that includes a cigar lighter, glare-reducing horn ring, bright-finish hubcaps, cab-compartment interior insulation, and cab rear quarter windows. A100 pickups with optional cab rear quarter windows are a joy to drive because of their excellent vision in every direction.

Left
Although an excellent little pickup, Dodge's A100 never achieved real sales success. For that matter, neither did compact pickups built by competitors. Dodge's A100 compact pickup, however, remained available longer than either Ford or Chevrolet's compact pickups. A100 pickup's maximum GVW rating of 5,200lb (2,160lb payload capacity) was nothing to sneeze at. Dodge's 318ci, 210hp optional V-8 engine had the muscle to easily move that weight and more.

nouncement was very much in keeping with Dodge's policy of introducing improvements when they were perfected, not necessarily at the beginning of a new model year.

To start with, dramatic appearance changes were made to front-end styling. The new look included a full-width grille consisting of five horizontal bars and three vertical bars. Dual headlights in use since 1961 were replaced by single headlamps. Wide chrome headlight rims seen on compact trucks for the past year were now used on all conventional cabs.

An additional appearance change was the adoption of a new full-length body side molding. This optional molding was bright metal with a paint-filled inset (white paint for dark body colors and black paint for light body colors). Series designation plates were relocated from the grille to both sides of front fenders.

The most important was the double-wall cargo box construction for all Sweptline models. Only Dodge offered a full-depth double-wall construction. The others used a double-wall which only extended two-thirds of the way up, leaving the top third an unprotected single-wall.

A new tailgate was wider (65in) and had a single latch, allowing the tailgate to be operated with one hand.

The A100 pickup featured one of the widest tailgates on the compact truck market. It opens up to a big cargo box that is more than 7ft long, over 5-1/2ft wide, and almost 2ft deep. Stake pockets for side panels allow for even more capacity. Yes, the spare tire is located where it was designed to be stored.

The A100's bright-finish hubcaps proudly display Dodge's Delta symbol in contrasting black paint. Optional full wheel covers, interestingly, did not have the Delta symbol.

Steel straps replaced the old-fashioned chains. Smart-looking new slim taillights complemented the wider tailgate. They gave the truck's rear a different appearance.

The growing popularity of pickup campers caused Dodge to extend the wheelbase lengths of half- and three-quarter-ton pickups from 122 to 128in. The added length gave better weight distribution and improved riding comfort. Another concession to pickup camper haulers was making the rear of the Sweptline box perfectly vertical. A new, larger 8ft box replaced the 7-1/2ft box on 128in wheelbase Utiline pickups in the half- and three-quarter-ton series. The short wheelbase half-ton pickup continued to ride on a 114in wheelbase.

Lack of production capacity was the only reason the U.S. truck industry did not have even a better year than it did. A record 1,785,109 units were built.

For the first time in history, the lightest truck class, under 6,000lb, reached one million units. Most trucks in this class were compacts.

Dodge enjoyed a good year. Production for 1965 increased 5.8 percent to 143,452, and sales increased by 19 percent to 116,639.

1966 Dodge B Series

Because Dodge trucks had been redesigned and re-engineered in midyear 1965, 1966 models carried over without change except for tweaking standard paint colors.

This year set the high-water mark in Dodge truck history in terms of total product offering. It seemed as if Dodge had a model for every trucking need from light-duties to heavy-duties. Never again would Dodge offer such a wide selection of models. This was the last year for Town Panel and Town Wagon, which were being capably replaced by compact vans and wagons. Dodge built 196 different models, ranging from half-ton to five-ton capacity.

Dodge posted a good year in 1966. Total industry production was off by about 20,000 units, but Dodge was

Standard engine was the 170ci, 101hp slant six. Optional was this 225ci, 140hp slant six. The engine's "dog house" was located fully within the cab centered between the bucket seats.

up by 6.8 percent to 153,159 units, which gave Dodge 8.7 percent of total industry production. Calendar year sales of 120,082 reflected a 3 percent increase over 1965.

1967 Dodge C Series

Because the current series trucks were only a year and a half old, no appearance changes were made in the 1967 models. Engineering-wise, the most interesting change was the addition of the 383ci, 258hp V-8 engine as an extra-cost option. Dealers had been hounding the factory for a larger engine to better handle the bigger, heavier pickup camper units coming into popularity and for more torque to pull ever-larger, heavier trailers. The 383 was the first engine released for truck service that wasn't specifically built for truck use. Engineering was satisfied that the horsepower and torque of the 383 was far in excess of any expected requirements; after all, the 383 was the most powerful pickup engine in the industry.

1968 Dodge D Series and 1969 Dodge E Series

Dodge light-duty and medium-duty models received a facelift late in the 1967 model year. The biggest change was in the bold new grille.

Also new for 1968 were sporty Adventurer half- and three-quarter-ton pickups. Standard features included carpeting, bright grille and exterior moldings, added insulation, hooded dials, dual armrests, wheel covers on half-ton D100s, and hubcaps on D200 pickups. Optional Adventurer features included mylar window trim, black or white vinyl roofs, bucket seats with center console, nameplates, and Delta emblems added to the Adventurer's sports look. A big standard full-width rear window for improved visibility was a new safety feature. The Custom Sports Special pickup model was discontinued in favor of Adventurer pickups.

The biggest change for 1969 was an eye-catching redesigned luxury instrument panel. For the first time, the automatic transmission control lever was mounted on the steering column. Also for the first time, factory air conditioning became an option and the redesigned instrument panel contained air conditioning outlets. A protective padding ran the full length of the panel. A new instrument cluster face plate, with edge lighting and rectangular shape, and a flip-up glove compartment door complemented the new dash design.

Adventurer models became even more luxurious and upscale with numerous luxury features added as standard or optional.

Custom chrome trim sets this half-ton short-box black beauty apart from ordinary pickups. It is an 18,000-mile, like-new, original-condition truck.

1970 Dodge F Series and 1971 Dodge G Series

In 1970, Dodge Truck management found it had created a winner with its Adventurer pickup. Truck buyers were willing to pay extra for appearance and convenience options. With a restyled grille, handsome exterior, and elegant interior, the 1970 model was the most stunning Adventurer of all time. Foam-padded, cloth-and-vinyl bench seat and full, color-keyed carpeting

Left
Dodge began in earnest to upgrade both exterior and interior appearance of pickups in the 1968 model year with an "appearance package" that added bright trim to the exterior and upscale interior appointments. For 1969, the trend continued with a Custom model, shown, and the first-ever Dodge Adventurer. The Custom dress-up package included a bright-finish grille, front bumper, fender opening moldings, rocker panel moldings, cab drip moldings, a Custom nameplate, and Dodge Delta hood ornament. A redesigned hood was also new.

were standard equipment. Passenger-car styling for passenger-car luxury, comfort, and prestige was Dodge Adventurer, the pickup specially built to lead a double life: always ready to work, always eager to play.

Second-Generation Compact Trucks

Making their initial public appearance in March 1970, second-generation 1971 Dodge compact vans and wagons featured a wind-tunnel body shape.

A major feature of the new van design was forward placement of front axle, engine, and front-end sheet-metal projection. The new design provided easy accessibility to the engine intrusion in the driver's compartment. The engine, which was removable through the front of the vehicle, was moved forward 24-1/2in.

Another significant new feature was the increased ease of driver entry and exit. Front wheels were moved forward 19in to allow the door openings to be placed more naturally behind the wheels. Doors were designed

Standard engines were the 225ci, 140hp slant six and this 318ci, 210hp V-8. The 383ci, 258hp V-8 was an extra-cost option. Note factory air conditioning equipment.

to provide larger, concealed step wells with less front wheelhouse intrusion.

New van and wagon models helped to confirm Dodge's leadership position in this important market segment; neither major competitor was even close to offering serious competition. In an effort to solidify its competitive position in the pickup market, Dodge Truck was poised to launch a completely new line of light-duty trucks in 1972. For this reason, 1971 light-duty models showed only a few cosmetic and engineering changes.

The Custom interior package added dash liner, glare-reducing trim around the instrument cluster, cigar lighter, color-keyed horn bar, and extra cab insulation. Note the original dealer-installed clear vinyl seat covers. Dash-integral air conditioning was another new feature for 1969. Also new was a steering column-mounted automatic transmission gearshift lever.

Chapter 8

Life-Style Pickups, T300, and Adult Toys and Vans 1972–1996

Light-duty Life-Style trucks were both good news and bad news for Dodge. Good in that they were well designed, comfortable, powerful, fun to drive, and as long-lived as any competitor's truck. The bad news came about because of what they were; as the name suggests, they were designed and engineered first for recreational and personal use, and second as work trucks. Travel and outdoor recreation were consuming the time and resources of a large percentage of Americans in 1972. Capable Dodge engineers succeeded in creating a truck that handled and drove like a car, possessed the interior comfort of a car, and whose inside and outside appearance rivaled car styling. However, Life-Style trucks were equally at home on the job. They were powerful, sturdy, and very able to haul or pull large loads on- or off-road. Frames, axles, brakes, transmissions, and engines were engineered in the best Dodge tradition for strength, reliability, and long life. Life-Style pickups worked as hard as former, tough, solid-axle Dodges, but with style and comfort.

Well then, what was the problem? Simply this, throughout the decade of the 1970s, Dodge heavily promoted light-duty trucks for recreational or personal use to the point of overdoing it.

Dodge Truck's long overdue full-size pickup sales turnaround began in 1989 with the introduction of the first Dodge Cummins turbo diesel-engine-powered pickups. The addition of the Cummins turbo diesel engine was such an obviously good idea that buyers flocked into Dodge showrooms with checkbooks in hand. Dodge Cummins was not just another participant in the light-duty diesel field, but a certified revolutionary new player. Dodge offered the Cummins diesel only in three-quarter-ton pickups, shown on left, and one-ton pickups, shown on right, as well as in one-ton chassis cab models. These trucks were photographed in August 1995 while attending the First Annual Turbo Diesel Registry Convention.

At this time, Dodge also led the industry in van and wagon sales. Dodge sold more van chassis for conversion to motor homes, more medium-duty chassis to motor home manufacturers, and more plain Jane vans to van converters than any other manufacturer.

Toward the end of the decade, Dodge marketing turned its attention to the "Adult Toys from Dodge." Admittedly, these were interesting and exciting trucks and vans, but they did nothing for Dodge's reputation for building tough work trucks. Many Dodge collectors today are thankful for high-performance Li'l Red Express Trucks, Warlocks, Macho Power Wagons, Four by Four Ramchargers, and Street Vans, but the market by and large did not see a connection between these vehicles and work trucks.

The final blow to Dodge Truck's tough work truck reputation occurred in 1979 when Chrysler management discarded all V-8 engines larger than the 360. A big engine with power and torque is critical to the success of a powerful light-duty work truck, especially for three-quarter and one-ton models that are normally purchased for work, not play. The same argument can be made for vans purchased for work use; Dodge vans, too, were hampered because they didn't have a big engine able to compete with the other members of the Big Three. Management sat on the sidelines and watched its full-size pickup market share almost slip below the waves. Fortunately, 1989 full-size trucks powered by Cummins turbo diesels came along just in time to revive Dodge's long lost reputation for power and the ability to get the job done better than anyone else.

1972 Dodge H Series

Design criteria for the H series trucks were "to incorporate more passenger-car-like comfort and convenience . . . with no loss of function of the vehicle as a truck." The entire line of light-duty trucks was redesigned to suit the

One-ton Power Ram W350 pickup identifies its Cummins engine on top of its fenderside four-wheel-drive nameplate.

Three-quarter-ton two-wheel-drive Ram pickup identifies its Cummins engine on the bottom of its fenderside nameplate. Both trucks also display a Cummins identifier on their tailgates.

recreational market for towing trailers and carrying campers or toppers. Changes were almost wholly in appearance and convenience, not in running gear. Engine option changes included dropping the 198ci slant six and 383ci V-8 and adding the 360ci, 180hp V-8 and the 400ci, 200hp V-8. Standard engines were either the 225ci slant six or 318ci V-8. The chassis, including new independent coil-spring front suspension, was new. Dodge's light-duty truck line was showing its age, but a restyled new cab, front sheet metal, and Sweptline cargo box freshened up its appearance and put Dodge back into the high-style pickup game. Wheelbase lengths increased to 115in from 114in for half-tons, 131in from 128in for three-quarter-ton models, and 135in from 133in for one-ton models.

Major cab interior updates included a wider cab and seat for more hip and shoulder room and larger windows for better vision and a more contemporary look. A modern dashboard with round recessed gauges to prevent glare was new. Doors were enlarged by 2in and opened wider than before to give better entry and exit.

Dodge managed to get these new trucks on the road after only three and a half years of planning, designing, engineering, and testing, and $50 million, a bargain by today's standards.

1973 Dodge J Series and 1974 K Series
Dodge Truck was not content with introducing the most important advance ever in pickup design in 1973, the Club Cab, but also introduced one of the most im-

portant new body designs in the light-duty truck business—Kary Van.

Dodge Truck's place in truck history as "the" industry's innovator will be forever secure based on the strength of the advancement represented by 1973's Club Cab pickup. At this point in time, adding 18in to the length of the cab doesn't seem like such a big deal, but it was in 1973. In fact, it still does to this day as Club Cab and its host of look-alikes from every other truck manufacturer continue to pull a bigger and bigger share of the pickup market. This was not an innovation asked for by owners or dealers; Dodge management sprung the Club Cab on the market. The strength of this new product was immediately demonstrated in sales numbers and profits.

Initially, Club Cabs were available only with two-wheel-drive trucks in half- and three-quarter-ton capacities. Wheelbase lengths were 133in equipped with a 6-1/2ft cargo box and 149in equipped with an 8ft cargo box.

Passenger-carrying capacity of Club Cab increased by adding optional fold-up jump seats mounted on either side of the cab, facing inward when in use. The rear area

Right
Chrysler Corporation's management and designers anticipated that the 1994 Ram pickup's styling was going to be of the "love it or hate it" type. As it turned out, however, the new Ram's styling was much more loved than hated; in fact, because of the new Ram, full-size pickup's styling will never again be the same. Dodge changed the rules for all others to follow.

offered the solution of where to store equipment away from the weather when leaving the vehicle unattended.

More late model year introductions were the Dodge Ramcharger and Plymouth Trail Duster twins. Originally, the Ramcharger was to be named the Laredo, but was changed before the introduction date.

Chrysler designed these two sport utilities as luxury off-road machines featuring a comfortable ride, pleasant appearance, attractive interiors, and an easy drive with automatic transmission, power assists, air conditioning, and other car-like amenities.

1975, 1976, and 1977 Dodge Trucks
(Series Designators Dropped with 1975 Models)

Dropping nonprofitable heavy-duty trucks was the major revelation for 1975. Club Cab pickups were selling so well and were so profitable, Dodge Truck management felt it was better to drop the marginally profitable heavy-duty trucks to concentrate on higher-volume products with wider profit margins. Medium-duty trucks with conventional cabs were retained, however. In fact, the line was expanded with the addition of D700 chassis cab and S700 school bus chassis models. These trucks were built in an exclusive plant in Windsor, Ontario, Canada.

Light-duty truck improvements were limited, but nevertheless significant. They included full-time four-wheel-drive models W100, W200, and W300. A New Process 203 transfer case was used with all available engines and transmissions. Power front disc brakes were standard equipment on all Power Wagons, and the huge 440ci V-8 engine option was broadened from two-wheel-drive trucks to all Power Wagon models. The Ramcharger lineup was expanded to include a two-wheel-drive option. It was not offered with the 440, however. All light-duty trucks—including two-wheel-drive and four-wheel-drive models, pickups, Power Wagons, and Ramchargers—were given a new instrument cluster for easier, quicker reading.

Dodge freshened up its 1977 pickup line with a new grille design. The change was simple but effective, giving light-duty trucks a fresh new appearance. A few minor interior refinements added to the cab's luxurious appearance.

1978, 1979, and 1980 Dodge Trucks

A diesel engine returned to power Dodge trucks for the first time since 1942, not in heavy-duty trucks, but this time in half- and three-quarter-ton pickups, and two-wheel-drive and four-wheel-drive models. The

Chrysler's designers broke new ground in truck styling by attaching the grille to the hood instead of to the body for easier access to the radiator.

diesel was the 6DR 50A, in-line six from Mitsubishi Motors Corporation, Chrysler's Japanese partner. It developed 103hp at 3700rpm from 243cid and 168lb-ft of torque at 2200rpm. Although it was a quality diesel, it suffered terminally from lack of performance and did not return for the 1979 model year.

Other than the diesel engine and a new D300 one-ton dually crew cab, only minor appearance and engineering changes were offered for 1978.

The story for 1979 was downsizing. For example, a new small D50 pickup imported from Mitsubishi Motors of Japan (with a Plymouth model included) was a new addition to the line. Second, Dodge Truck's engine line was severely downsized. Gone were the diesel, 361ci, 400ci, 440ci, and 413ci V-8 engines. Gone also were all medium-duty trucks and light- and medium-duty motor home chassis. The only products remaining were pickups up to one-ton, vans and wagons up to one-ton, and the two- and four-wheel-drive Ramchargers. Sadly, it was the beginning of a new era in Dodge truck's long history.

The biggest change in Dodge pickups for 1980 was a part-time four-wheel-drive system that replaced full time four-wheel-drive to aid fuel economy, reduce weight, and reduce drivetrain noise. Considerable change was in store for 1981 pickups. Management held changes, appearance, and engineering for 1980 down to a bare minimum.

1981 to 1993 Dodge Trucks

Dodge trucks entered a new era in 1981: the Iacocca era. Lee Iacocca became chairman late in 1978, and this was the first redesign of the nine-year-old full-size truck platform since he arrived. Management positioned D/W trucks as "better values" or as "good values."

An important component of its value story was price, which we see more of beginning in 1982 with the full-size D150 Miser pickup. Dodge provided a whole menu of convenience and comfort options to attract customers. One of Iacocca's early decisions was to revive the concept of the Dodge Ram, which had been a symbol of Dodge toughness and durability since the early thirties. He then instructed Dodge advertising to push the concept of Ram truck toughness and durability. A sculptured Dodge Ram symbol was proudly positioned on the hood of every 1981 Dodge pickup, chassis cab, and Ramcharger.

Because of the nation's energy consciousness, Dodge heavily promoted the economy of six-cylinder engines with four-speed manual overdrive transmissions, or a 5.2ltr V-8 engine with manual overdrive transmission for those who required additional performance. Dodge truck's engine line was simple: 3.7ltr slant six, 5.2ltr and 5.9ltr V-8 engines. Slant six was equipped with a single-barrel carburetor; the 5.2, with either a two-barrel or four-barrel; and the 5.9 with only a four-barrel carburetor.

Dodge fielded a full line of light-duty trucks: standard cab, Club Cab, and crew cab full-size pickups with either Utiline or Sweptline cargo boxes; chassis cabs; three sizes of full-size vans and wagons; two-wheel-drive and four-wheel-drive Ramcharger full-size sport utility vehicles; and new best-selling D50 mini pickups imported from Mitsubishi.

Joseph Campana became the company's new general manager for truck operations in 1982. He came to Chrysler from Ford, and before that he was a GM new-car dealer. His job description called for him to revive Chrysler's ailing truck business. His goal was to capture Chrysler's share of the truck market. Campana came to Chrysler three years earlier as director of marketing

Dodge led the industry in getting heavy-duty jobs done with Magnum-powered three-quarter and one-ton trucks. They were powerfully equipped to tackle big jobs with industry-leading Magnum V-10 gas or Cummins turbo diesel engines. The 1996 one-ton V-10 Ram 3500 4x2 Laramie SLT Club Cab pickup with dual rear wheels was America's most powerful pickup. Its 300hp and 450lb-ft torque out-muscled all other pickups including the Dodge Cummins turbo diesel. Owners confidently and safely towed legal GCWR loads of 19,000lb as a practical matter, however, many owners routinely exceeded this limit. *Chrysler Corporation*

Dodge's largest-in-class cab featured the most hip, head, and shoulder room, and a true three-big-man 40/20/40 bench seat. The center armrest/business console, shown folded up, offered generous storage space for an owner's laptop computer, cellular phone, and any amount of miscellaneous items.

plans and programs. From there, he moved to general manager of truck operations in 1982. His major efforts to recapture truck market share in 1982 included launching the car-based front-drive, front-engine Rampage pickup, the four-wheel-drive Power Ram 50 mini pickup, and the D150 Miser pickup, America's lowest priced full-size pickup selling for only $5,899. It was powered by a standard slant six engine and five-speed manual transmission and was positioned in the marketplace to compete with minitrucks. The initial year of production for both Chevrolet's S-10, GMC's S-15, and Ford's Ranger small pickups was 1982. Club Cab models were dropped with the end of production in 1981. Full-size pickup sales declined in 1982 while sales of the new U.S.-built small trucks boomed. Japanese-built small truck market share fell to only 50 percent in 1982 (they previously owned the entire small truck market).

Left
Ram's 1500 half-ton Sport for 1996 was built for the legions of buyers who purchase pickups for personal transportation. This black beauty was as comfortable at a posh country club as it was parked outside of the office. Sports were available in several colors, but black was the standout finish.

The Sport's standard engine was the 5.2ltr Magnum V-8; a 5.9ltr Magnum V-8 was a no-cost option.

The Li'l Red was the flashiest of the three supertrucks; trim items included tape striping, chrome exhaust stacks, and real wood. Li'l Red's nose sits a bit lower because its front wheels are one-inch smaller than its rear tires. For that reason, Li'l Red Trucks were not equipped with a spare tire.

Dodge dropped the Utiline cargo box late in the 1985 calendar year. Labor-intensive Utiline boxes were not economical to build due to their hand labor construction versus robotic welded Sweptline boxes. Chevrolet and Ford soon followed suit. Ramcharger

Left
While not a cataloged Adult Toy from Dodge, the late-in-the-model-year Li'l Red Express Truck was considered an Adult Toy. When entered against a 454-powered GMC pickup and a 460-powered Ford pickup in a contest to find the top muscle truck for 1978, the Li'l Red with its li'l 360 walked away the winner, hands down. Not only that, but the Li'l Red was the lowest priced of the three supertrucks, and it delivered the best gas mileage. Li'l Red Express earned its well-deserved reputation as, "The Last American Hot Rod," honestly.

production was moved to Mexico in the fall of 1985. Interestingly, Ram pickups were the corporation's top-selling nameplate for model year 1985. The most notable engineering advancement for 1985 was the addition of a new vacuum-actuated front inner-axle connect-disconnect "Ram Trac" system. It enabled the driver to shift to and from four-wheel-drive mode with the vehicle in motion at speeds up to 55mph.

The pickup's appearance was freshened up for 1986 with a restyled grille and front and rear bumpers. To make room for the new Dakota, launched on October 2, 1986, as 1987 model trucks, Dodge shortened its full-size truck offerings to three-man cab Sweptline pickups and chassis cabs only.

A four-wheel-drive version of the new Dakota mid-size pickup debuted in the spring of 1987. Extended

What goes up these fully functioning bright chrome dual exhaust stacks comes out of a basic police interceptor engine. The 360 has a camshaft designed for a high-performance 340 V-8, a set of 340 valve springs, stock cylinder heads, and a Carter Thermo-Quad carburetor with a low-restriction air cleaner.

wheelbase minivans were new for 1987, as was the imported Dodge Raider sport utility. An important historical event occurred in 1987: Chrysler Corporation purchased Jeep from American Motors.

The engineering advancements of note for 1988 included dropping the veteran 3.7ltr slant six from full-size pickups, vans, and wagons and replacing it with the 3.9ltr V-6 engine originally developed for the Dakota. To achieve greater power and performance from the 3.9ltr V-6 and 5.2ltr V-8 engines, single-point throttle body fuel injection became standard equipment.

The excitement that began in 1989 with the addition of the Cummins diesel engine option continued into 1990 when Dodge announced a Club Cab version of its popular Dakota midsize models. And, not only that, but Club Cab options for full-size D/W half- and three-quarter-ton pickups returned. Dakota Club Cabs were built in Dodge City, but full-size Club Cabs were

built in Mexico along with Ramchargers.

Performance took on a deeper meaning in 1992 for full-size Dodge Ram pickups, vans, and wagons. More powerful, redesigned 3.9ltr V-6 and 5.2ltr V-8 Magnum engines, as well as upgraded drivetrains, complemented the increased horsepower of these two powerplants, which joined Dodge's world-class Cummins intercooled turbo diesel. Horsepower for both the 3.9ltr and the 5.2ltr V-8 engines was dramatically increased over prior years—45 percent for the V-6 and 30 percent for the V-8. Torque increases were also substantially improved. Both engines included sequential multipoint fuel injection management systems. A redesigned, heavy-duty four-speed automatic transmission was paired with the 5.2ltr V-8 in all Ram pickups to enhance performance, fuel economy, and durability. A new, heavy-duty five-speed manual was mated to either the 3.9ltr V-6, the 5.2ltr V-8, or the 5.9ltr V-8 in Ram pickups, vans, and wagons.

A Magnum 5.9ltr joined the two smaller Magnum engines in 1993. In early January 1993, at the Detroit International Automobiles Show, the Dodge T300 pickup was unveiled to the world's automotive press corps. The last D/W pickup was built in early May 1993, and T300 production began in June 1993.

1994 to 1996 T300 Dodge Trucks

The Corporation invested $50 million in its 1972 Life-Style models and $1.2 billion in its new T300 models. This seems like a lot of money, but when compared to the $1.3 billion the Corporation spent on its new Neon compact car, it was a genuine bargain.

"The rules have changed," boasted Dodge Truck advertising when promoting its first new full-size pickup in twenty-two years. By that they meant they had "rewritten the rules on what pickups could offer." Dodge set the T300 apart from competitors' trucks. It had a tough big-truck exterior look and designed-in ruggedness, yet it coddled driver and passengers with smooth, quiet engines; an industry-first air bag; two- or four-wheel anti-lock brakes; passenger car-like-ride, steering, and handling; the industry's largest cab loaded with comfort features including modular storage behind the seat, and a 40/20/40 split bench seat which featured a designed-in office with space for a cell-phone, computer, pencils, pens, and writing pads.

The only carry-over items were its Magnum engines, which included the 3.9ltr V-6; 5.2ltr and 5.9ltr V-8 engines, and the Cummins 5.9ltr turbo diesel engine. Early in 1994, Dodge added the 8.0ltr V-10 with 300hp and 450lb-ft torque to compete against the big block V-8s from GM and Ford. The V-10 was the industry's most powerful pickup engine, even more powerful than the Cummins diesel. V-10-powered pickups were genuine, died-in-the-wool work trucks targeted for the really big jobs; not for running to the Quick Stop for a quart of milk.

Adult Toys: Pickups and Vans, 1977–1980

Based on when Dodge officially introduced its first "Adult Toy," we would have to peg the year the Adult

The powerplant of the Li'l Red was not Dodge's largest, but it didn't lack for performance. Standing one quarter-mile time was 15.7 seconds at 85mph, and top speed is estimated at 125mph!

Toy era began as 1976. Adult Toys, however, were more of a lifestyle than a product. It is interesting to note that Dodge considered its trucks of this era, 1973–1980, Life-Style trucks. Beginning early in this decade, buyers began to seriously shift buying patterns from automobiles to light-duty trucks and vans. By 1976, Dodge vans and pickups were undergoing a complete change—from commercial to personal use. More than 40 percent of the trade-ins for vans and pickups were cars. Dodge van and pickup sales were exploding. Month-to-month sales increases over the year before ranged from 50 percent to over 100 percent. The same was true, of course, for other manufacturers, but Dodge owned the biggest share of the van market.

Dodge Truck's restyled, re-engineered 1971 compact vans and 1972 pickups played a major role in this market shift. Converted vans became a new lifestyle among the young. Hippies probably started the movement in the 1960s with their outrageous Volkswagen vans. Van conversions of the 1970s, while related, were entirely different from a hippie's van. The 1970-era vans were more sophisticated, larger, more powerful, and much more roadworthy.

Four-wheel-drive pickup and sport utility sales exploded along with sales of vans and two-wheel-drive pickups. Industry four-wheel-drive sales in 1976 boomed 45 percent over those of 1975. Sales of four-wheel-drive vehicles, which had formerly been primarily sold in mountain states and areas with heavy winter snowfalls, had spread to all areas of the country by 1969–1970. Sales of four-wheel-drive pickups were taking about 26 percent of sales versus only 13 percent six years earlier.

Several aftermarket conversion firms converted stock two-wheel-drive vans to four-wheel-drive. The Big Three looked at making them a factory option, but four-wheel-drive vans sales never hit the big time.

The new Dodge Street Van went on sale for the busy spring selling season in March 1976. A Street Van amounted to nothing more than a do-it-yourself truck finishing kit. Street Vans were a variant of Dodge's commercial Tradesman van. To hold prices down, Dodge did

The 1978 Dodge half-ton Macho Power Wagon was a Sweptline pickup with rugged four-wheel drive and tough good looks. The Macho Power Wagon's distinctive appearance was backed up by a powerful 318ci V-8 engine; 10-15LT-B wide, deep-tread tires; and choice of 115in or 131in wheelbase configurations. Standard paint design was red, black, and orange. *Chrysler Corporation*

as little of the customizing as possible at the factory. That was left to the buyer with help from the factory.

Street Vans were shipped painted one solid exterior color. Included with the Street Van were exterior trim suggestions from Chrysler stylists, along with an assortment of other aids for adding designs and figures to the basic paint job.

Interior equipment intended to appeal to the active young person who made up the fast-growing market for customized vans included deluxe instrument panels with woodgrain inserts, bright instrument clusters, deluxe door panels, woodgrained horn bars, cigarette lighters, carpeting, and high-back bucket seats with fold-down armrests in cloth and vinyl. Exterior equipment included bright grille surround, bumpers, windshields, taillamps, side mirrors, fat H70x15-B tires with raised white letters, and five-slot chrome disc or painted spoke road wheels.

A special Customizing Kit gave owners a wealth of ideas for complete personalization, including exterior paint designs and color combinations, interior plans that included full-sized paper templates with instructions and photographs for step-by-step use, instructions for adding sound systems, lists of suppliers for options, and the names of major accessory manufacturers.

Dodge tailored trucks to handle specialized jobs as well, as pickups and vans with special trim and option packages in 1976 set one sales record after another. Dodge built a run of trucks with special trim and accessories for the Los Angeles market and a different truck for the San Francisco area. Dodge sales in 1976 were 126,000 units ahead of 1973, the former record sales year.

The 1976 special Dodge truck for the Los Angeles area was the first Warlock. It was cataloged and sold nationwide in 1977. Dodge management spotted the exploding interest in customized half-ton pickups and gave buyers a factory-built specialty truck with all the goodies buyers wanted, including performance and handling upgrades. Dodge saved buyers all the extra work and time of building a special truck and still priced the Warlock favorably.

Chrysler Corporation gathered the automotive press together in mid-1977 at Ontario Motor Speedway, Ontario, California, to introduce them to an expanded line of Adult Toys. Vehicles shown included the Warlock, Macho Power Wagon, Street Van, and Four by Four Ramcharger/Trail Duster.

Dodge/Plymouth management told the automotive press corps representatives the company was well aware of the truck boom and was seeking to create "adult toys" for a great many pickup, van, and four-wheel-drive enthusiasts, or in other words—big toys for big boys. The company's strategy was to "market vehicular identity, with names, custom paint, stake racks, pinstripes, big tires, roll bars, and exciting interior appointments, all either factory installed, or bolted/painted on by high-volume contract customizers." Corporate engine/drivetrain lineups remained unchanged. Chrysler took the plunge and entered the trick-truck market with optional factory personalization of utility vehicles for the recreation-oriented buyer.

Evidently, Chrysler hit the nail on the head, for the auto writers liked what they saw and drove. One writer said, "Dodge and Plymouth vehicles reflect the hard-core enthusiasts' hearts' desires—quickness, strength, controllability, and capability for a variety of utilitarian and fun-trucking tasks. With the paint and custom trim options, Chrysler will hit one group in the buying market; and corporate manufacturing of very acceptable trucks will hit the other; and maybe paint plus power will hit some of each."

By 1978, the light-duty truck market had shifted to one which was almost 50 percent for personal use. "Pickups filled more than just a basic transportation need; buyers were not looking for a motorized wheelbarrow, they were looking for personalized fun vehicles," said Al Umber, manager of truck sales for Chrysler Corporation.

Therefore, Dodge Truck fielded in 1978 the line of Adult Toys first presented to the automotive press in mid-1977 in Ontario—Street Van, Warlock, Macho Power Wagon, and Four by Four Ramcharger/Trail Duster.

The Ramcharger Four by Four was another of the 1978 Adult Toys from Dodge. This sure-footed Adult Toy was designed to take on the unbeaten path in style. The Ramcharger Four by Four was equipped for rough going with a muscular 318ci V-8 engine. Big 10-15LT-B tires fitted to painted spoke or chrome disc road wheels, power front disc brakes, electronic ignition, and a five-setting transfer case were standard equipment. High-back command seats were a luxury option; a three-passenger rear bench seat with twin armrests was also an extra-cost option. *Chrysler Corporation*

Dodge's most exciting, interesting, and long-lasting favorite, the Li'l Red Express Truck, was a late model year introduction, not hitting the streets until spring 1978.

As if Dodge's line of Adult Toys was not enough, early in 1978 Dodge added another line of custom off-road vehicles. Both GM and Jeep already had similar programs in place. Chrysler's version was called the Top Hand series. The program worked like this: buyers could go into a Dodge showroom and order all the decor items needed to make their vehicle special, then lump the cost into their monthly payment. The buyer did not have to contend with the manual labor of installing parts. The custom items came in the form of packages and, in the case of the Top Hand, the accessories used were all from one manufacturer.

Ordering a Top Hand was a matter of working with a local dealer, picking out the package that best suited the buyer's needs, and ordering a vehicle from the factory. The factory dropped the ordered vehicle at a special facility where the Top Hand package was installed. The Top Hand packages were from Hickey Enterprises, and the parts used in the package, with the exception of lights and paint, were Hickey products.

Chrysler offered the Top Hand in its full vehicle line: Ramcharger, Trail Duster, Sweptline, and Utiline pickups (both two- and four-wheel drive).

Typical options included paint decor design; steel spoke wheels painted matching colors; front-end grille guard; chrome tow hooks; two Cibie lamps; three-spoked, leather-wrapped steering wheel; roof rack; tie downs; and 3in roll bars with three lights. All lights were wired and ready to use.

Or, high-rollers could order the Sidewinder III 9,000lb front-mounted power winch, bed rails, folding steps, axle trusses (front and rear), a rear spare tire, and dual gas can rack for Ramchargers and Trail Dusters.

Dodge's entire set of Adult Toys, including the Li'l Red Express but with a D50 Sport model added, returned for 1979. They all included regular 1979 model styling and engineering updates, of course. Unfortunately, one of the engineering updates included deleting all big block, high-performance engines.

Adult Toys came to an end with the 1980 model year when the only Adult Toys models remaining were the Street Van, Macho Power Wagon, and D50 Sport.

Not all Warlocks were painted black. Warlock offered a choice of six exterior colors with lots of special gold accents inside and out. Fancy chrome disc road wheels or painted road wheels were standard equipment. Other standard equipment included real oak sideboards, chrome-plated mini running boards, and dark-tinted glass all around. Warlock was available in either two-wheel or four-wheel-drive models, but always only on the 115in wheelbase chassis with Utiline cargo box. Powerplant choices included the 225ci Super Six or 318ci V-8 engines. *Chrysler Corporation*

The 1990 Li'l Red Express Dakota is certainly not as well known as the original Li'l Red Express of 1978, but it is nevertheless an interesting little truck. Unlike the original Li'l Red, the Dakota-based Li'l Red Express was not built by Dodge Truck. It is a creation of L.E.R. Industries of Edwardsburg, Michigan. L.E.R. Industries purchased complete Dakota pickups, removed their factory cargo box, replaced it with a fiberglass short cargo box with metal liner, and added dual chrome-plated exhausts, accent logo package, special wheels and tires, and tube-type rear bumper.

The original Li'l Red Express featured genuine wood-trim panels on its tailgate versus the Li'l Red Dakota's decals.

The Li'l Red Express Dakota's cab interior is a totally stock Dakota LE interior with bench seat.

Left
All of the bed liner's steel parts, including its floor, are constructed of Galvineel, which is virtually unaffected by corrosion. The outside parts of the cargo box are either aluminum or fiberglass. Top surfaces of the flat flares are aluminum covered.

Dodge's 1964 compact truck line—van, Sportsman wagon, and pickup—offered more quality and value than compact trucks from competitors. Dodge Truck had its back up to the wall in 1964 and was battling to survive. Management knew these vehicles had to be best-in-class if Dodge Truck was going to continue as a viable competitor. Being the last player to enter the game has its advantages, and Dodge played its cards perfectly. The marketplace agreed by voting with its pocketbook. Dodge compacts sold well immediately upon arrival at dealerships. *Chrysler Corporation*

Chapter 9

Vans and Small Pickups
1964–1996

During the second half of the 1950s and the early years of the 1960s, Dodge truck sales were in the pits. Dodge Truck's market share in 1952 was 13.1 percent, which was in line with average yearly market share figures dating back to the mid-1930s, but percentages began falling in 1953 and continued to fall through 1961 when market share hit a low of 6 percent. A 54 percent loss of market share should send a signal to management that strong medicine was needed immediately to correct a very sick situation. Chrysler management issued an ultimatum to the Truck Division, "Either improve market share or shut it down!"

Ford and Chevrolet's new 1961 compact trucks, designed to compete with Volkswagen's van, wagon, and pickups, were introduced in the fall of 1960. Dodge designers and engineers closely studied these three manufacturer's compact trucks before beginning design work on a line of Dodge compact trucks. They concluded that Ford's compact was the best of the lot, a position confirmed by sales figures. While Ford's compact was a worthy competitor, Dodge engineers felt confident they could build a better series. And they did.

The 90in wheelbase Dodge A100 compact van was more powerful, more attractive, sturdier, capable of hauling heavier loads, featured bigger wheels and tires, offered more comfortable seats and a wider array of optional equipment than all other compacts, and was the lowest priced. Dodge's 1964 A100 compact trucks may just be the most important new introduction in Dodge's history. More important than 1994's T300 pickup? Look at it this way: without the A100, would Dodge Truck have been around in 1994? A100s gave way in 1970 to the new, larger second-generation B series vans, which took more than 50 percent of the van and wagon markets during the 1970s. The reputation for durability, dependability, and utility earned by these two important products of the 1960s and 1970s cer-

tainly helped Chrysler's 1984 minivans become Chrysler's most important product of the 1980s. Minivans have been rightly credited as saving the company from oblivion and creating a whole new market category in the automotive industry. Chrysler, since 1984, has held onto minivan leadership with the fury of a female Alaskan Kodiak bear protecting her newborn cubs. Chrysler's minivans were in no small part responsible for the market's shift to trucks, vans, sport utilities, and minivans in the late 1980s at the time when it appeared that Japanese-built automobiles were about to make toast of America's automotive industry. The Japanese have never been able to successfully compete against American-built truck products. Minivans not only saved Chrysler, they were the principal contributor in saving America's auto industry!

Of the three A100 products—van, wagon, and pickup—the van was the most important in terms of sales, accounting for over 50 percent of compact sales. The A100 pickup was an interesting product, well built, well designed, powerful, and without question capable of hauling, but the market never voted so with orders. For that matter, no other compact pickup fared very well. Compact wagons sold well, but not quite as well as vans. Interestingly, compact wagons were officially tallied as automobiles, not as trucks, even though they were built in the truck plant along with vans and pickups.

It would appear as if customers considered wagons cars. Customers preferred six-cylinder engines over V-8s in pickups and vans, but chose V-8 engines over sixes in wagons, which was more or less true in general for cars versus trucks.

Dodge vans became the vehicles of choice for America's businesses—delivery trucks, tradesmen's trucks, and a whole host of other specialized functions. Dodge planned it that way by offering the industry's widest range of options and special equipment, allowing customers the freedom to

Dodge's 1982 Rampage pickup, based on the compact Dodge Omni automobile, was built in an assembly plant along with Omni and Horizon cars. It was the first, and only, front-wheel- drive Dodge pickup. Rampage seemed like a good idea, and the company tried real hard to sell this truck, but sales never took off forcing the company to drop it after the 1984 model year.

customize a van to their particular needs. Vans were offered in two distinct types, with or without side doors. Doors could be installed in one or both sides as well as the back. The second version was called a panel van. Panel vans had doors only in the rear, with or without windows. Most buyers preferred to have side windows, at least on the right side for better vision while driving in traffic.

Dodge's industry-leading compact trucks received a boost in 1967 with the addition of the A108 king-sized van and wagon. The A108 van's extra 18in body offered 10ft of sheltered, flat cargo space, or with the passenger seat removed, 14ft of load space for extra-long items. The van's wheelbase was also stretched an extra 18in for a balanced ride. The extra cargo area, amounting to 43 additional cubic feet, was added between the stretched wheels, not in rear overhang.

Dodge introduced its 1971 line of compact Tradesman vans and Sportsman wagons (no pickup) in the spring of 1970. Dodge engineers took a clean sheet of paper and started from scratch to design their second-generation vans and wagons.

Major features of the new design was forward placement of front axle, engine, and front-end sheet metal projection. The new design provided easy access to the engine compartment from the front and reduced engine intrusion in the driver's compartment. The engine was moved 24-1/2in forward.

Dodge was slow to discontinue the term compact from these vehicles, which were no longer compact. New maximum GVW ratings increased to 7,700lb compared to a former high GVW of 5,400lb. Cargo floor lengths also increased; floor length was now 117.3in from engine cover to rear door.

New wheelbases were either 109in or 127in. Interior loading space was 206cu-ft and 245cu-ft, respectively. Three models comprised the new line—B100, B200, and B300—with half-, three-quarter-, and one-ton capacities, respectively.

The base slant six engine was increased to 198ci. An optional engine was the 318ci V-8.

Front wheels were moved forward 19in to allow the door opening to be placed more naturally behind the wheels for increased ease of driver entry and exit. Doors were designed to provide larger, concealed step wells with less front wheelhouse intrusion.

New vans and wagons were just right for America because sales of these versatile new vehicles exploded almost immediately, selling 2.4 times that of the first-generation vans and wagons.

Small Pickups

Dodge Truck's first-ever small truck came at just the right time; actually, earlier would have been better, but later would have been pure disaster. Ford and Chevrolet began selling imported minitrucks in 1972. Their small trucks arrived in time for the first energy crisis, Dodge's not until the second energy crisis.

Chrysler's Dodge D50/Plymouth Arrow pickups were designed and built in Japan for Chrysler by Chrysler's Japanese affiliate, Mitsubishi Motors Corporation. The truck came in two forms—Standard and Sport. Wheelbase on both was 109.4in, cargo box was 6-1/2ft long, and payload was 1,400lb. Both trucks featured roomy cabs, with plenty of seat travel and extra-wide doors, but the Standard came with a plain interior and a 2ltr (122ci) four-cylinder engine, while the Sport was delivered with an upscale interior and a 2.6ltr (156ci) four. Power was 93 and 105hp, respectively, but both featured Silent Shaft counterbalancing and the MCA Jet exhaust emissions control system. The Sport, in addition to a flashy exterior, also had an upgraded interior that featured bucket seats and floor carpeting instead of bench seats and rubber mats. The Standard truck came with a four-speed manual transmission; the Sport came with a five-speed manual transmission. An automatic was optional with either.

Both trucks had a smooth, almost passenger car-like styling. Not so noticeable, but equally important, was their good ride from an A-arm front suspension and beam-axle rear suspension. Coil front springs and variable-rate leaf springs at the rear were standard. Power front disc brakes and rear drum brakes were also standard. A long list of optional equipment was offered with both models. Chrysler promoted the D50/Arrow as "the bigger little truck, the quietest, quickest, roomiest." All-in-all, Chrysler's dynamic-duo were fine little trucks, which the corporation badly needed, and thankfully, they sold extremely well in a highly competitive market.

Dodge Truck added its first small four-wheel-drive pickup, the Power Ram 50, in 1982. Two price classes were offered: Power Ram 50 Custom and Power Ram 50

Chrysler began importing minitrucks from Mitsubishi Motors Corporation in 1979. These trucks were well engineered, well designed, and became an immediate sales success. Shown here is a 1982 Dodge four-wheel-drive Power Ram 50.

Sport, both with a 2.6ltr four-cylinder engine and five-speed manual transmission.

Power Ram 50s had torsion-bar independent front suspensions with A-shaped unequal upper and lower control arms and front stabilizer bar. Torsion bars allowed a more compact front suspension design and resulted in a smoother ride off-road.

Dodge Truck's first American-made small truck, and the first front-wheel-drive pickup built by a member of the Big Three, literally combined the comfort and convenience of a passenger car with the utility of a pickup and a load capacity of 1,140lb.

The Rampage was built on the Dodge Omni platform and shared the car's front styling, front-wheel drive, and its improved Trans-four 2.2ltr engine, which produced 84hp at 4800rpm.

Built on a wheelbase of 104.2in, the sporty new truck had an overall bumper-to-bumper length of 183.6in, stood 51.8in high, and had an outside width of 66.8in. It was offered in two models: High-Line and Sport.

Unitized construction combined body and frame into a single structure for greater strength and rigidity without adding weight that might detract from the handling or fuel economy. And because it was welded, rather than assembled with nuts and bolts, the Rampage was built to remain solid and tight for many thousands of miles.

Dodge Ram 50 for 1983 was the only small pickup featuring a turbo diesel engine in the North American market. It was designed to deliver the best performance of any light truck available, while maintaining the superior mileage of a diesel.

The new diesel was a 2.3ltr four-cylinder with Silent Shaft and was offered as an option in Dodge Ram 50 pickups from Mitsubishi Motors. It was available only with a five-speed manual transmission. Turbocharging increased horsepower 25 percent, yet maintained high fuel mileage and smooth performance. It produced 80hp at 4200rpm and 125lb-ft of torque at 2600rpm. Mileage targeted was 34mpg in city driving for the two-wheel-drive models and 30mpg for the four-wheel-drive model.

The Rampage pickup was dropped at the end of the 1984 calendar year.

Technically, Dodge Dakota is a midsize truck and the only one in its class. It provides the muscle of a full-size truck and the sporty appearance usually associated with smaller compact trucks. When introduced in 1987, Dakota was offered in two wheelbase lengths with either 6-1/2ft or 8ft cargo boxes. Since 1987, a four-wheel-drive Dakota, Club Cab models, and a V-8 engine option have been added. This is a 1987 top-of-the-line Dakota LE.

Dodge Caravan C/V (C/V for conversion van and cargo van) for 1989 was agile and responsive in city traffic. On the highway, it cruised smoothly and quietly thanks to its car-like front suspension and, new for 1989, 3.0ltr EFI V-6 engine. Practical-minded owners found thousands of uses for Caravan C/V's 160cu-ft of cargo space. Hauling firewood was one of the more unusual, however.

This engine is a 218ci, 75hp L-head six-cylinder which powered the 1937 half-, three-quarter-, one-, and one and a half-ton trucks. Clutch, transmission, and emergency brake are attached behind the engine. The physical layout of this engine is typical of most L-head Dodge truck engines in service from 1933 to the late 1960s. This engine family was well known for dependability and low cost of operation. From the left side of the engine a driver could service the radiator, check the oil level and add oil, check the brake fluid level, and lubricate and service the distributor, water pump, and starter. Only the carburetor and manifolds were located on the engine's right side.

Chapter 10

Engines

From 1918 on, Dodge truck engines were corporate automobile engines modified for truck service. The extent of modifications depended upon the service they would be subjected to. For example, an engine destined for a half-ton pickup would be modified only slightly, probably no more than adding a chromed top piston ring for extra long life. On the other hand, a big V-8 engine built for medium- and heavy-duty truck service was extensively re-engineered and contained many premium features. Dodge truck engines were and are built as truck engines on separate manufacturing lines and carry engine numbers distinct from car engines, even though they may look identical.

A truck's engine is its single most important component. Trucks are built for one purpose: to move the biggest possible load from point A to point B in the shortest time at the lowest cost. Many, maybe even most, trucks sold in the past twenty years have been sold for personal transportation and almost never carry a load heavier than the family sedan carries; but our primary concern here is with work trucks.

The early sales success of Dodge Brothers commercial cars was due in large part to the reputation earned by Dodge Brothers automobiles for dependability and low cost of operation. The same Dodge Brothers four-cylinder engine that powered those automobiles powered one-ton and one and a half-ton Graham Brothers trucks beginning in 1921 and through the two-ton trucks in 1926. These bigger trucks were also an immediate sales success due to the sterling performance of their Dodge engines. Dodge's four-cylinder engine was larger and more powerful than four-cylinder engines used by its two major competitors—Ford and Chevrolet.

Dodge Brothers commercial car sales (from 1918 on) and Graham Brothers truck sales (from 1921 until the company was sold to Chrysler in 1928) were limited only because the huge Dodge Brothers manufacturing complex was unable to build all the cars and trucks buyers were willing to purchase.

Based in large part on its excellent engine, Dodge established itself as the industry leader in performance and became the benchmark for all competitors to strive for.

With the 1929 model year beginning on July 1, 1928, which happened to be the same time that Walter Chrysler purchased the company, the famous Dodge four was no longer used in any Dodge automobile. Dodge had switched its entire car line over to six-cylinder engines. For the 1929 model year, Dodge trucks from the smallest half-ton to the largest three-tonners were six-cylinder powered. Graham Brothers began building a three-ton truck in 1928 because of the availability of the Dodge 242ci, 78hp L-head six-cylinder engine.

Dodge Truck's Chrysler era began, unfortunately, with the worst economic depression this country has ever known. As a way to become more price competitive in the 1930s economy, where too many truck builders chased too few truck sales, Dodge trucks again offered a four-cylinder engine. It was the Plymouth L-head four with 174ci and 45hp inherited from Maxwell Motors Company, the company which Mr. Chrysler used as a springboard to form his own Chrysler Motors Company in 1925.

Chrysler also brought to the table two big engines for Dodge Truck use. Interestingly enough, both were originally Chrysler Imperial engines. In 1930, a 310ci six making 96hp was added exclusively for three-ton trucks. With later increases in displacement all the way up to 413ci, this engine stayed in the line until 1955. After 1930, it was never again used in an automobile.

The second large Imperial engine added for truck service was the 385ci, 115hp L-head straight eight, which was being used in Chrysler Imperials. Dodge Truck used it to power a new line of monster four-ton models. It stayed in the line only through 1934. Four-ton trucks did not sell well during the depths of the Depression.

Dodge's first trucks designed and engineered by Chrysler Engineering appeared in 1933. These new trucks were as new as could be; even their engine line had been designed by Chrysler engineers. In 1933, Dodge Truck began its tradition of powering its lightest trucks with Plymouth and Dodge engines, its medium-duty trucks with a Chrysler engine, and its biggest trucks with the big 310ci L-head six. However, that year was an exception in that a DeSoto engine was used in place of the Chrysler engine, but this was only a one-year situation. The big Imperial straight eight continued for four-ton models through 1934. A straight eight was never used in a Dodge truck after 1934. Chrysler's entire six-cylinder line, with the exception of the 310 big block, was new for 1933. These basic engine blocks, although with larger displacements from time-to-time, remained in the line powering Power Wagons through 1968.

Chrysler set the industry back on its heels in 1939 when it introduced its own diesel, designed, engineered, and manufactured in-house. It shared the same displacement as the big block six-cylinder gas engine, which made it appear to be the same engine warmed over for diesel use, but that was not true. Dodge Truck engineers designed its block similar in size to that of the gas engine simply for manufacturing economies, as both engines were installed in three-ton trucks. Inside, however, the diesel was ruggedly built with heavy components, as a diesel should be. The diesel was installed in trucks through 1942; however, they were built during World War II for the military for industrial applications.

Dodge Truck re-entered the four-ton market in 1950 by increasing the size of the big block L-head six to 377ci and adding dual carburetors and dual exhausts. This was the first time dual exhausts and carburetors were offered as factory-installed equipment on any Dodge truck engine. By 1953, Dodge offered dual carburetors and exhausts on its 265ci, 306ci, 331ci, and new 413ci L-head sixes.

Quite possibly one of the most interesting periods in Dodge Truck's engine history was the Hemi era of 1954 to 1959. In some respects it paralleled the Cummins 5.9ltr turbo diesel era, which began in 1989 and continues to this day. Dodge introduced an engine whose performance was so far superior to anything in the industry that buyers immediately recognized that fact and instantly began to snap them up. Hemis were the darling of the independent owner/operator who ran one or a small fleet of either straight trucks or tractors. These operators were able to purchase, at a very reasonable price, Dodge trucks that would run rings around all competition. Hemis were able to quickly accelerate to highway speeds and then run down the road fully loaded at top legal speeds with nary a slowdown for hills. Owners realized top profits by making more runs per day than owners operating competing brands.

Dodge offered three Hemi engines in 1954: a small 241ci engine with a single one-barrel carburetor for one and a half-, two-, and two and a half-ton trucks; a 331ci engine with single one-barrel carburetor for two and three-quarter- and three-ton trucks; and a second 331 with a two-barrel carburetor for three and a half-ton trucks. The 413ci big block six with dual carburetors and dual exhausts was in its second year, and it alone powered four-ton trucks.

The Hemi lineup for 1955 remained much the same except the smallest Hemi was a 270ci for two and a half-ton trucks only. The two 331 Hemis remained as before.

Dodge became serious about Hemis in 1956. The smallest was the single-barrel 331 in two and a half-ton-ners, then the 331 with dual carburetors and dual exhausts for three-ton trucks, and finally a 354 with dual carburetors and dual exhausts for four-ton trucks. By developing 354lb-ft of torque, the 354 Hemi became the first Dodge truck engine to develop 1lb-ft of torque per cubic inch displacement, a claim few, if any, other gas-powered engines could make.

In 1959, the last year of the Hemi era, a 315ci Hemi was offered for two- and two and a half-ton trucks, plus three versions of the 354—with single-barrel carburetor, two-barrel carburetor, and dual carburetors and dual exhausts for three- and four-ton trucks.

When Dodge Truck began its Heavy-Duty Diesel Truck era in 1960, Hemis were dropped (Dodge Truck used Hemi engines one year longer than cars did) and were replaced by a new family of high-performance V-8 engines. They included the 318 (Dodge Truck's first 318 appeared in 1959; the 1960 version was a premium-built model), 361, and 413 V-8s with premium components. Note that V-8 engines for medium- and heavy-duty trucks were offered in several forms. For example, in 1960, three 361s—361-2, -3, and -4—were available with horsepower ratings ranging from 178 to 204 and maximum torque ratings ranging from 291 to 335lb-ft. The larger the dash number, the more premium components were engineered into the engine. Also added to the line for heavy-duty trucks were four Cummins diesel engines.

In the minds of many, the most interesting family of engines ever in Dodge trucks was introduced in 1961—170ci and 225ci slant sixes. Two years later, engineers added a medium-duty version of the slant six, the premium-built 225-2, which replaced the ancient 251 L-head six in medium-duty models. Premium features included roller timing chain, stellite-faced valves, bi-metal connecting rod bearings, and polyacrylic valve stem seals.

To provide greater power for the new, bigger compact vans of 1970, the 170ci slant six was dropped in favor of the more powerful 198ci slant six.

The only car engine Dodge ever added to its truck line without specifically adapting it for severe service was the 383ci V-8 in 1967. Dodge engineers felt this engine had far more horsepower and torque available than it would ever be called on to use; therefore, it did not require premium components to stand up to the rigors of light-duty truck service.

Dodge began to slowly add additional V-8 engines to its light-duty line in the early 1970s. First, the 360 in

1972 for vans and pickups, and the 400 for pickups only. The 225-2 premium slant six was dropped in 1972.

In 1974, the huge 440 V-8 was made available for light-duty trucks and motor homes, and the 400 was relegated to service in Ramcharger and Trail Duster only.

A number of more powerful Cummins diesel engines, including V-8 models, were added subsequent to 1960. In addition, Detroit Diesel and Caterpillar diesels were also offered. The small Perkins diesel became an option for medium-duty city delivery service. All diesel engines were dropped in 1975 when Dodge got out of the heavy-duty truck business.

Nineteen seventy-eight was an interesting year because Dodge added its first-ever light-duty diesel engine for half- and three-quarter-ton pickups only. The Mitsubishi-built 243ci six-cylinder diesel did not sell well and was eliminated after only one year.

The bottom fell out of Dodge Truck's engine line in 1979 when management dropped all engines larger than the 360ci V-8 due to the nation's second energy crisis.

After an absence of many years, Dodge again offered four-cylinder-powered trucks in 1979, the Mitsubishi-built mini D50 pickups.

Dodge labored through the 1980s with only three engines for full-size trucks, the 225 slant six, 318 V-8, and 360 V-8; however, the rules changed in 1989 when the first Dodge Cummins turbo diesel-powered trucks hit the street. Suddenly Dodge was again the hottest truck in town. It outpulled, outcarried, outperformed, and outmuscled everything in sight. Not only that, but it delivered better fuel mileage, longer life, and lower operating costs.

The last chapter in Dodge Truck's engine history is the world's first V-10. Dodge engineers chose V-10 engine architecture over a big V-8 or V-12 because it is not as long as a V-12, and the big bores of a large V-8 tend to cause pre-ignition problems in a hardworking truck engine. More small cylinders give more performance because greater valve area per cubic inch displacement makes for better breathing, and the smaller cylinders control pre-ignition problems. Even though Dodge's Viper shares a V-10 engine, the V-10 was developed first for truck use. At 450lb-ft of torque, the V-10 is far and away the light-duty truck torque and performance champion. No competitor can touch it.

It is a tradition with Dodge Truck engineers to outpower competitors. For example, at the time this book was published, Dodge truck engines were the envy of the industry. The Cummins intercooled turbo diesel is the undisputed king-of-the-hill, and Dodge intends for it to remain so. Dodge's industry-exclusive V-10 gas engine has even more horsepower and maximum torque than the Cummins. These two engines cover the full-size truck field most adequately, while the Magnum 318 V-8 rules in trucks smaller than full-size, including the mid-size market segment, which Dodge Dakota owns all by itself.

Dodge Truck engineers one-upped the competition in 1992 with their new Magnum gasoline engines. Magnum engines retained their former piston displacements, but inside, Magnum engines were wholly new. "Magnum" specifically referred to modernizing with nineties technology in computer-controlled multipoint fuel injection, which resulted in huge increases in horsepower and torque outputs, better fuel economy, and quantum increases in lowering exhaust emissions. In the first year, only the 3.9ltr V-6 and 5.2ltr V-8 engines were re-engineered; the 5.9ltr V-8 followed the next year. Four years later, the other guys re-engineered their truck engines.

Going back a few years, Dodge dominated the first-generation compact truck market, first with the largest six in the field. Second, it introduced the first and only V-8 engine in 1965 with the small 273ci V-8, and in 1967 replaced it with the 318ci V-8, which was still the only V-8 in the compact truck market.

Possibly the most outrageous factory-optional engine ever installed in a Dodge pickup was the high-performance engine for the 1964 and 1965 Custom Sports Special pickups. Rated horsepower was 365 at 4800rpm, and maximum torque was a whopping 470lb-ft at 3200rpm. The high-performance engine package required rear axle struts, dual exhausts, three-speed Load-Flite automatic transmission, power steering, and a heavy-duty instrument cluster with tachometer. Buyers were warned that any signs of abuse would void their warranty. Its 10.3 to 1 compression ratio required the use of premium gasoline. But a buyer could drive from the showroom to the drag strip and almost be guaranteed a trophy. A 1965 half-ton 128in wheelbase Sweptline pickup sold for $1,881.00, the Custom Sports Special package for $255.30, and the high-performance package for $1,235.60. Now you know why 426-powered Custom Sports Special pickups are a rare sight.

Index